Table Talk *for the Experienced*

Further Conversations About the Ross Periodic Table

Second Edition

Jim Ross

 *London Ontario Canada*

National Library of Canada Cataloguing in Publication	Ross, Jim (James William), 1952-
	Table talk for the experienced: further conversations about the Ross periodic table / Jim Ross.
	1. Chemistry, Organic--Textbooks. I. Title.
	QD253.2.R68 2013 547 C2013-901333-3
Author	Jim Ross
Printer	CreateSpace
Cover Design	Jim Ross

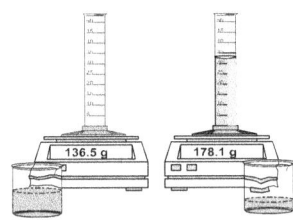

© Copyright 2013 by Ross Lattner Educational Consultants.

All rights reserved. The use of any part of this publication, reproduced, transmitted in any form or by any means, electronic, mechanical, photocopying, recording or otherwise, or stored in a retrieval system, without the prior consent of the publisher, is an infringement of the copyright law and is forbidden.

Permission is granted to the individual teacher who purchases one copy of *Table Talk 2nd Ed.*, to reproduce the student activities for use in his / her classroom only. Reproduction of these materials for an entire school, or for a school system or for other colleagues or for commercial sale is strictly prohibited.

ISBN	978-1-897007-05-1
Offices	London Ontario Canada

To teachers, parents and students everywhere who desire to bring about new ways of understanding the world.

I welcome your comments and suggestions. Let me know what you find most useful.

I've worked hard to remove any errors. Still, don't let a day go by without letting me know if you find one.

Stay in touch.

Jim Ross

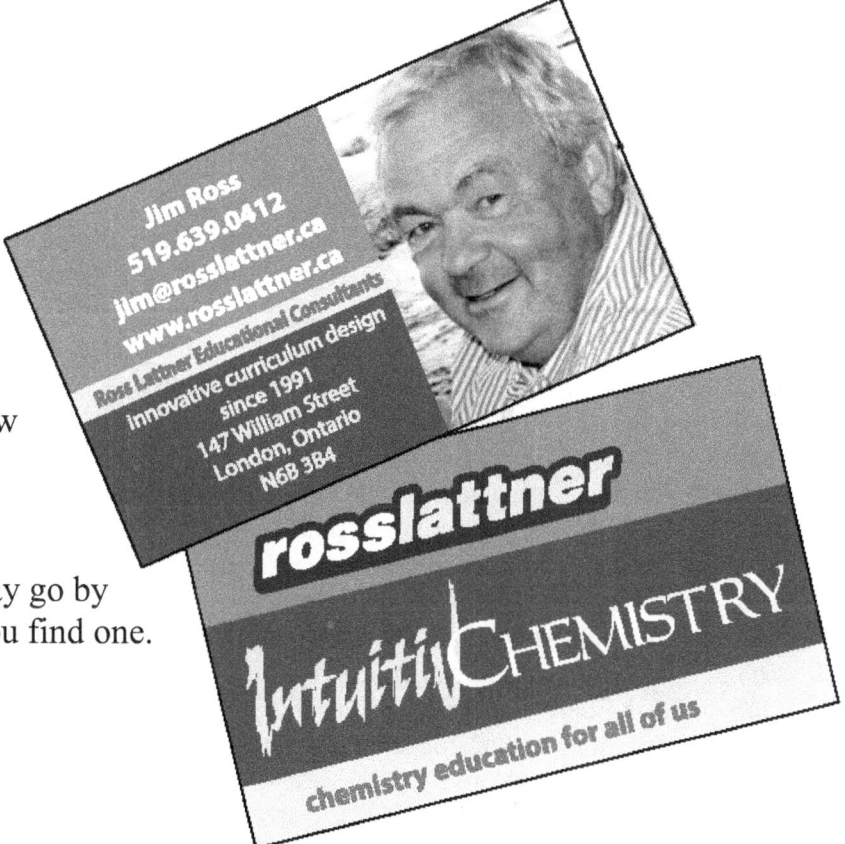

To Dick Bird, my own senior chemistry teacher. A man at once skeptical and passionate, Mr. Bird inspired two generations of chemistry students in Belleville, Ontario to do better than had been done before.

Table of Contents

Parents and Teachers Guide and Resource 1

Activity 1.2: Gaining Electrons is Reduction 4
Activity 1.3: Losing Electrons is Oxidation 5
Activity 1.4: Determining Formal Oxidation Numbers 6
Activity 1.5: Elements With Multiple Oxidation Numbers 7
Activity 1.6: Oxidation Numbers in Common Polyatomic Ions 8
Quiz 1: Oxidation States 9
Activity 2.1: The Essential Concepts of Redox Reactions 10
Activity 2.2: Redox Reactions Between Metals and Non-Metals 11
Lab 2.3: Redox Reactions Among Non-Metal Elements 12
Lab 2.4: Redox Reactions Among Covalent Molecules 13
Quiz 2: Redox Reactions 14
Activity 3.1: Carbon and Hydrogen 18
Activity 3.2: Oxidation Numbers in Hydrocarbons 19
Activity 3.3: Oxygen and Nitrogen in Organic Molecules 20
Activity 3.4: Redox Reactions of Organic Molecules 21
Quiz 3: Oxidation and Reduction in Organic Chemistry 22
Activity 4.1: Electron Potential Energy 24
Activity 4.2: The Combustion of Non-Metals 25
Activity 4.3: The Spectacular Combustion of Metals 26
Activity 4.4: The Combustion of Methane 27
Quiz 4: Electrons and Energy 28
Lab 5.1: The Strange Dipolarity of Water 30
Lab 5.2: Alcohols as Dipoles 31
Lab 5.3: Carbonyl Groups as Dipoles 32
Quiz 5. Polar Bonds and Dipole Molecules 33
Lab 6.1: Reactions of Non-metal Oxides and Water 36
Lab 6.2: What Makes Non-metal Oxides Acidic? 37
Lab 6.3: Reactions of Metal Oxides and Water 38
Lab 6.4: What Makes Metal Oxides Basic? 39
Activity 6.5: Oxidation and Acid Strength 40

Table of Contents

Student Exercises and Labs 43

Activity 1.1: Gaining Electrons is Reduction 44
Activity 1.2: Losing Electrons is Oxidation 46
Activity 1.3: Determining Formal Oxidation Numbers 48
Activity 1.4: Elements With More Than One Oxidation State 50
Activity 1.5: Oxidation Numbers in Common Polyatomic Ions 52
Quiz 1: Oxidation States 54
Activity 2.1: The Essential Concepts of Redox Reactions 58
Activity 2.2: Redox Reactions Between Metals and Non-Metals 60
Activity 2.3: Redox Reactions Among Non-metal Elements 62
Activity 2.4: Redox Reactions among Covalent Molecules 64
Quiz 2: Redox Reactions 66
Activity 3.1: Carbon and Hydrogen 70
Activity 3.2: Oxidation Numbers in Hydrocarbons 72
Activity 3.3: Oxygen and Nitrogen in Organic Molecules 74
Activity 3.4: Redox Reactions of Organic Molecules 76
Quiz 3: Oxidation and Reduction in Organic Chemistry 78
Activity 4.1: Electron Potential Energy 82
Activity 4.2: The Combustion of Non-Metals 84
Activity 4.3: The Spectacular Combustion of Metals 86
Activity 4.4: The Combustion of Methane 88
Quiz 4: Electrons and Energy 90
Activity 5.1: The Strange Dipolarity of Water 92
Activity 5.2: Alcohols as Dipoles 94
Activity 5.3: Carbonyl Groups as Dipoles 96
Quiz 5: Polar Bonds and Dipole Molecules 98
Lab 6.1: Reactions of Non-metal Oxides and Water 102
Activity 6.2: What Makes Non-metal Oxides Acidic? 104
Lab 6.3: Reactions of Metal Oxides and Water 106
Activity 6.4: What Makes Metal Oxides Basic? 108
Activity 6.5: Oxidation and Acid Strength 110
Quiz 6: Acids and Bases 112

The Ross Periodic Table

+1 2.1								+2 --
+1 1.0	+2 1.5		+3 2.0	+4 2.5	+5 3.0	+6 3.5	+7 4.0	+8 --
+1 0.9	+2 1.2		+3 1.5	+4 1.8	+5 2.1	+6 2.5	+7 3.0	+8 --
+1 0.8	+2 1.0		+3 1.6	+4 1.8	+5 2.0	+6 2.4	+7 2.8	+8 --

© Ross Lattner Educational Consultants   147 William Street   London Ontario Canada   N6B 3B4   519-639-0412   www.rosslattner.ca

Parents and Teachers Guide and Resource

Why do we need another periodic table?

The Ross (**c**ore - **v**alence - **r**adius) periodic table is *designed for learners*. It helps beginners achieve a deep and dynamic understanding of chemistry right from the start. Why is the Ross table so effective? The Ross table is designed to match the way that human beings make sense of their environment.

First: Do kids think like little scientists?

What is a schema? Why is it meaningful?

How *do* students think about a new experience? Previous experience cannot be sufficient: in a new experience, they have nothing to go on. It can't be memory, since none exists. It can't be some kind of rule-based program, like a decision tree, or a flow chart. The time to make sense of the experience would be far to long, and the outcome far too unpredictable.

We are introducing our students here to a new idea: atoms attract electrons to themselves and in the process are "reduced." Our students do not think like scientists, and do not approach this new situation in the same way that a scientist would. This raises a general question of great importance. How *do* they think through a new scientific concept?

In this book, we propose that the first strategy that a student uses to comprehend any new situation is to apply a *schema*, a simple structure with inherently meaningful relationship among its parts. A *schema* is a gestalt structure, whose meaning lies in its whole, rather than its parts.

Two of the basic schemata used by students (of all ages!) are the *source-path-goal* schema and the *effort* schema.

Second: Human beings find meaning in schematic thinking before they find meaning in disciplinary thinking.

When human beings encounter novel events, we reason schematically. Only later do we learn to reason formally.

Linguists and cognitive scientists have identified schematic reasoning as one of the deepest and simplest ways that we make sense of the wold. Schematic reasoning is so fundamental to us that we hardly know we are using it. For example, dogs, cats and mice "know" that more effort provides more results. That's the *Effort Schema*. Humans use it, too.

Beginners use the *effort schema* to their advantage when they apply it to chemical concentration: more chemical provides greater concentration. Greater concentration provides greater results. Beginners are misled by the *effort schema* when they apply it to LeChatelier's principle.

The Ross table anticipates the student's use of schematic reasoning; students who use the effort schema with the Ross table can make scientifically defensible predictions. Successes, like rabbits, are prolific when they come in pairs.

What is a schema? Why is it meaningful?

Some cognitive scientists depict brain activity, including thinking, as the wave-like propagation of neuron activity over the surface of the brain. There is some speculation that abstract thinking may involve constructive and destructive interference of such "thought-waves." It may be that teenagers do not activate as many neurons and connections, and therefore cannot resolve more than four or five waves without losing or confusing them.

Chemistry is a challenge to beginners because of the sheer number of concepts involved. A prudent science teacher will limit the number of variables that the student must entertain.

In the Ross table, variables are limited to three: the core charge, the valence electrons, and the radius of the valence shell. Most students can make excellent judgements about the relative behavior of elements, based upon just those three variables.

Third: Students' schemata are the science teacher's greatest competition. They are also the teacher's greatest ally.

For all teachers and parents, the students' use of schemata is both our greatest competition and our greatest ally. This is especially the case when we wish our students to learn something new.

Students will use schemata whether we like it or not. If we fail to appreciate that fact, then students will skip whatever we are saying and rely upon their own schemata for their own personal sense of meaning about this new experience.

If, on the other hand, we carefully construct our lesson plans with the students' schemata in mind, we can provide the student with learning exercises that are closely tuned to their own natural sense of "the meaning of things." bring students to decision points in which s are

The Ross Periodic Table and the related exercises are designed to do just that. We propose here a way of representing the chemical behavior of atoms so that student's schematic intuitions lead to correct predictions. With the students' schemata on our side, we can bring the students to a deeply satisfying mastery of chemistry.

Let's begin.

Oxidation Numbers ...

Parents and Teachers Guide and Resource

Source Path Goal Schema

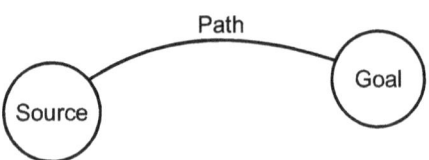

Proximity Schema

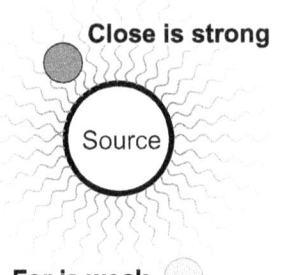

Close is strong

Far is weak

Activity 1.2: Gaining Electrons is Reduction

Pedagogical Issues We are pursuing a very traditional chemistry learning outcome in activities 1.1 to 1.4. We want our students to use the concepts of *oxidation number*, of *reduction* and of *oxidation* to analyze and to explain a wide variety of chemical phenomena.

We begin with reduction. In this way, we can make good use of two of the students' schemata. When the teacher represents core charge and radius as salient features of the atom, students can use the *proximity* schema to predict the attractive force upon nearby electrons. They use the source-path-goal schema to anticipate a reasonable trajectory of the electron.

Science Issues Because there is no universal symbol for oxidation number, we propose a new symbol: ∅ . It contains graphic references to oxidation, is easy to draw, and is not easily confused with any other symbol in common use in chemistry.

Two features of the Ross table are the core charge of an element, and its valence electron population. Rather than memorize a static set of oxidation numbers, students can predict oxidation numbers reliably from the Ross representation.

	(+7) Fluoride	∅ = (+7) + (-8) = -1	Fluoride F^-
	(+6) Sulfide	∅ = (+6) + (-8) = -2	Sulfide S^{2-}
	(+5) Phosphide	∅ = (+5) + (-8) = -3	Phosphide P^{3-}
	(+6) Oxide	∅ = (+6) + (-8) = -2	Oxide O^{2-}
	(+5) Nitride	∅ = (+5) + (-8) = -3	Nitride N^{3-}

... Oxidation is Losing

Ideas About Science and Pedagogy

- Oxidation is loss of electrons.

- Reduction is gain of electrons.

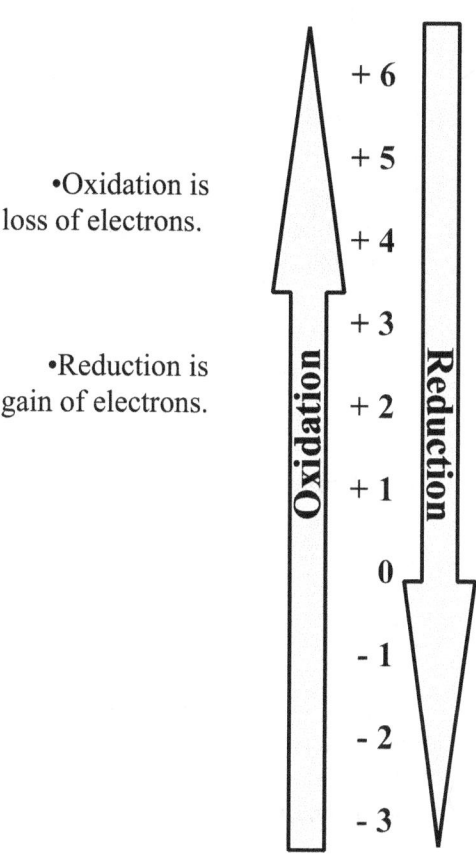

Activity 1.3: Losing Electrons is Oxidation

Pedagogical Issues Oxidation and reduction are not intuitive terms. Kids naturally think of oxidation as "combining with oxygen." If we teachers introduce and reinforce that idea early, we will have great difficulty introducing the more subtle concept later. In this exercise, the metals lose their electrons to fluorine, not oxygen.

The arrow graphic can be a help to students.
Increasing oxidation is up
Reduction is down.

Science Issues the arrow graphic at left is capable of including both "oxidation number" and the older "oxidation state."

The concept at this point is not very refined. Students will identify oxidation state with ionic charge, a necessary base camp from which we should depart as soon as possible.

[diagram]	Mg^{2+} (+2)	∅ = (+2) + (0) = +2	Magnesium ion Mg^{2+}
[diagram]	Al^{3+} (+3)	∅ = (+3) + (0) = +3	Aluminum ion Al^{3+}
[diagram]	Li^{+} (+1)	∅ = (+1) + (0) = +1	Lithium ion Li^{+}
[diagram]	Ca^{2+} (+2)	∅ = (+2) + (0) = +2	Calcium ion Ca^{2+}
[diagram]	Ga^{3+} (+3)	∅ = (+3) + (0) = +3	Gallium ion Ga^{3+}

© Ross Lattner Publishing   www.rosslattner.ca

Oxidation Numbers ...

Activity 1.4: Determining Formal Oxidation Numbers

In the past thirty years, research in science education has emphasized the acquisition of concepts. It might be time to re-examine the role of skills in science education.

Pedagogical Issues A subtle interplay exists between acquisition of skills and the acquisition of concepts within each individual student. Students are unlikely to "acquire a concept whole." A concept like "oxidation number" is first learned in a rough and uncertain form, then shaped and refined by many experiences.

A student is likely to first identify *oxidation number* with *ionic charge*. This first concept is true, but of limited value. The skill of calculating formal oxidation number provides the student with the tools to extend and refine the concept. The Ross model of the atom is readily compared with the formal calculation, so that the student has the means to independently test and confirm his or her understanding.

Students often appear to accept the fact that they may not fully understand a concept. The same students can become much more upset if they lack the skills to operate with that same concept.

Science Issues "Oxidation number" is a formality, but an important one. If we broaden the term "losing an electron" to mean "having an electron move away from," then we have the ability to use one concept to address metals, ionic bonds, non-metals, covalent bonds, and many forms of coordinate bonding in the transition metals.

1. H_2S +1 −2	5. P_4O_{10} +5 −2	9. $KMnO_4$ +1 +7 −2	13. PO_4^{3-} +5 −2
2. SO_2 +4 −2	6. H_2SO_4 +1 +6 −2	10. HCN +1 +2 −3	14. NO_2^- +3 −2
3. NH_3 −3 +1	7. K_2SO_3 +1 +6 −2	11. ClO_3^- +5 −2	15. CO_3^{2-} +4 −2
4. NO_2 +4 −2	8. $NaNO_3$ +1 +5 −2	12. SO_3^{2-} +4 −2	16. IO_4^- +7 −2

... Multiple Oxidation Numbers

Ideas About Science and Pedagogy

Activity 1.5: Elements With Multiple Oxidation Numbers

Students can become highly indignant when a teacher suggests that there is more than one possible "answer" to a question.

Pedagogical Issues Students often find the case of multiple oxidation numbers to be very difficult. They tend to apply one of two strategies to problems of this sort. Students either:

1. attempt to memorize a fixed set of possibilities
2. attempt to find a fixed set of rules to generate the possibilities.

In both cases, they run the risk of learning a limited short-cut to "the right answer," rather than achieving understanding of the problem.

The Ross table presents the atoms as players in a competition for electrons.

Science Issues Consider a phosphorus atom in the presence of an excess of fluorine. The elements P and F are competing for possession of each others' electrons. If fluorine is able to take possession of **one** of phosphorus' unpaired electrons, it is probably able to take all three. (Phosphorus ∅ = +3)

If enough fluorine is present, the additional fluorine can "split" the last pair of electrons on phosphorus, and then involve those electrons in bonds. (Phosphorus ∅ = +5)

1. Phosphorus and fluorine 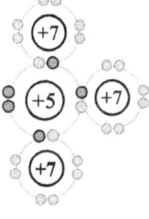	2. 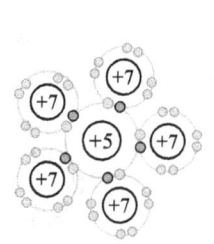 ∅ = +3 ∅ = +5
3. Oxygen and hydrogen ∅ = -2 ∅ = -1 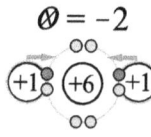	4. Tellurium and chlorine ∅ = +2 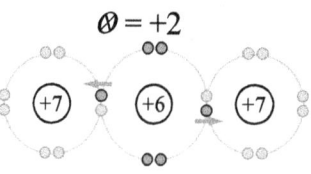
5. ∅ = +4 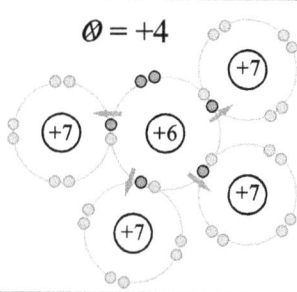	6. Sulfur and fluorine 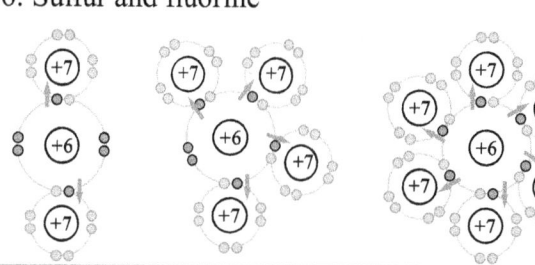

© Ross Lattner Publishing   www.rosslattner.ca

Oxidation Numbers ...

Activity 1.6: Oxidation Numbers in Common Polyatomic Ions

Experts see more possibilities than novices do. What learning strategies can teachers employ to help their students move from novice to expert?

Pedagogical Issues Students are novices, while scientists are experts. What makes the difference between a novice and an expert? One of the differences noted in educational studies is that novices tend to see a situation from one perspective, while experts have learned to "see" a situation through several representations. This presents a learning challenge to novice students, and to their teachers: what representations and what skill sets should we teach, to provide our students with two or three different perspectives from which to tackle the problem of oxidation numbers?

One strategy is to provide the student with several representations, and the skills to use them. In that way, the student can skillfully approach a problem with two or three distinctly different representations.

Chemistry textbooks use two common representations to solve the problem of oxidation numbers in polyatomic ions. The first representation is a system of "book-keeping" rules for oxidation numbers (see Activity 1.3). Novice students who use this method to obtain the bottom-line oxidation state may not understand *why* the atoms acquire a particular oxidation state. The second representation system is a set of rules for Lewis dot diagrams. A novice student can use these rules to tell *where* the electrons will be, while not understanding the dynamics that drive such systems.

The Ross table provides a representational system with dynamic properties. Novice students skilled in Ross diagrams can explain the dynamics driving the oxidation numbers in covalent molecules.

All of these representations provide novice students with useful insights, but none of the representations is literally true.

Science Issues The novice student who uses these representations must at the same time learn one of the deepest values of the science community: *coherency*. Each representation can be used to interrogate the others. When the three representations provide a coherent model of bonding, the novice student can be more confident of the resulting model.

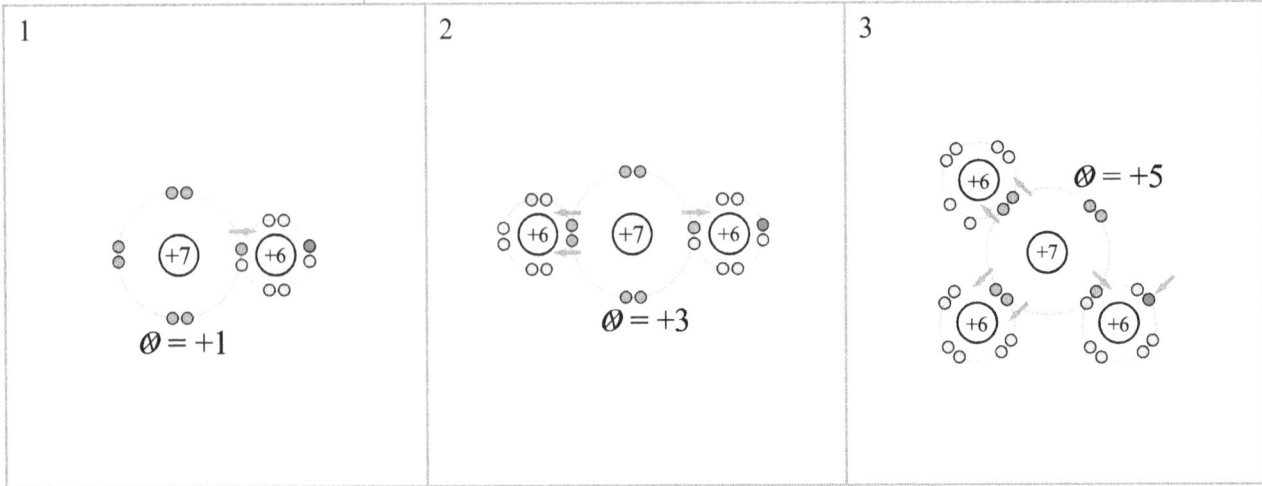

Quiz

Ideas About Science and Pedagogy

Quiz 1: Oxidation States

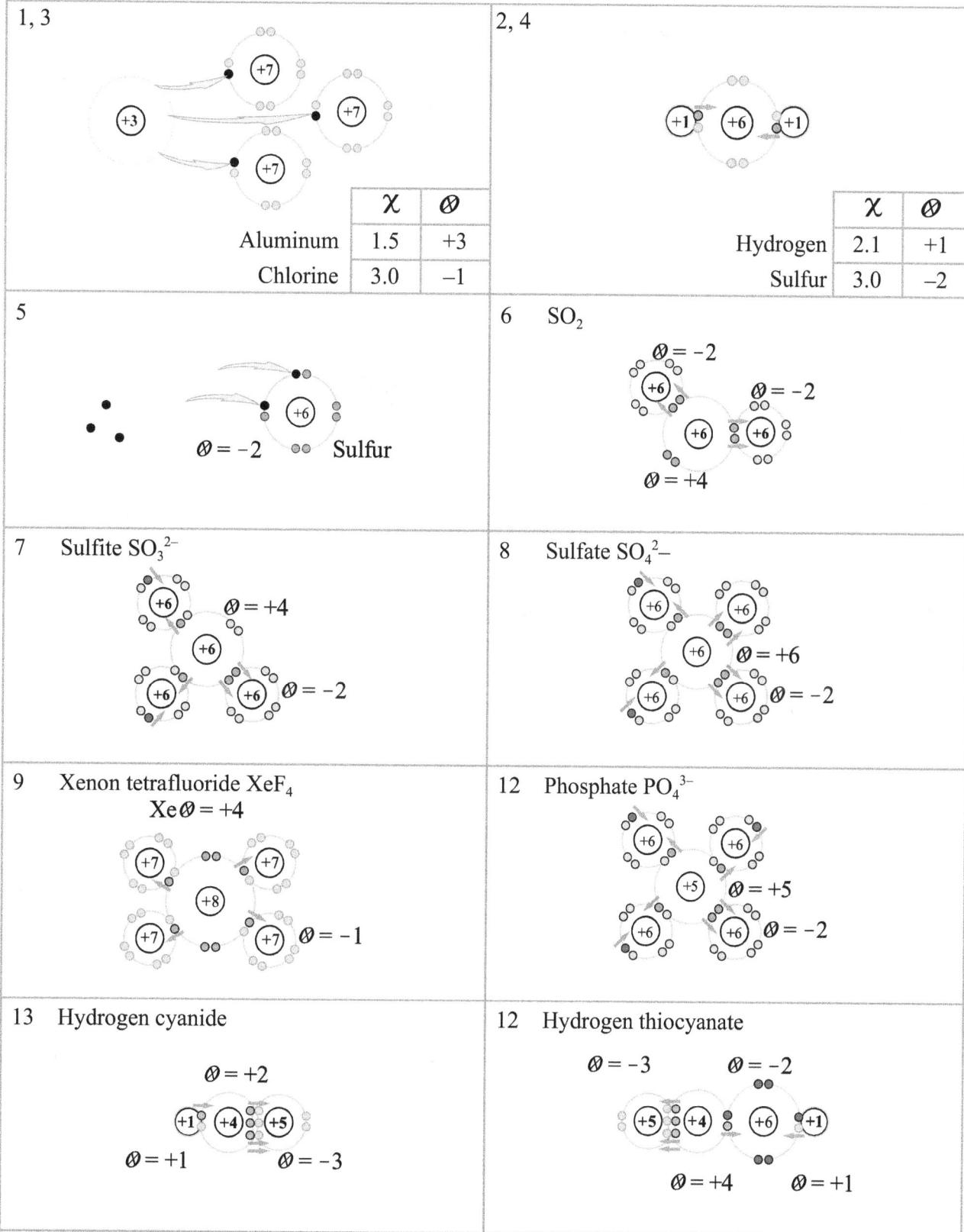

Redox Reactions ...

Suppose we describe an "idea" as an expanding wave of neuronal excitations, that echos and re-echos from fissure to fold across the cortex. When two "ideas" interact, we might think of two superimposed waves propagating in their characteristic patterns. Such a system would create an entirely new pattern of interference, a kind of dynamic hologram that ebbs and flows in its own way.

How many such "idea waves" can the human brain support? There must be an upper limit at which the interference pattern swamps some of the original "idea waves," pushing them out of awareness.

Activity 2.1: The Essential Concepts of Redox Reactions

Pedagogical Issues There is a limit to how many ideas a human being can keep going at one time. The limit is widely accepted to be about six or seven for adults, less for adolescents, and still less for children.

The concept of a redox reaction involves at least nine simultaneous ideas: lose electrons, oxidized, oxidizing agent, gain electrons, reduced, reducing agent, negative charge, positive charge, oxidation number, plus all of their attendant processes.

The complexity of a redox reaction, in other words, can easily overwhelm the human mind. As they struggle to learn this system, adolescents need some form of permanent representation to keep the ideas before them. In that way, they can "see" one part of the system as it connects with the others, even as the whole is still too large for their brain to encompass.

Science Issues this convention system is widely used around the world. We will build upon it.

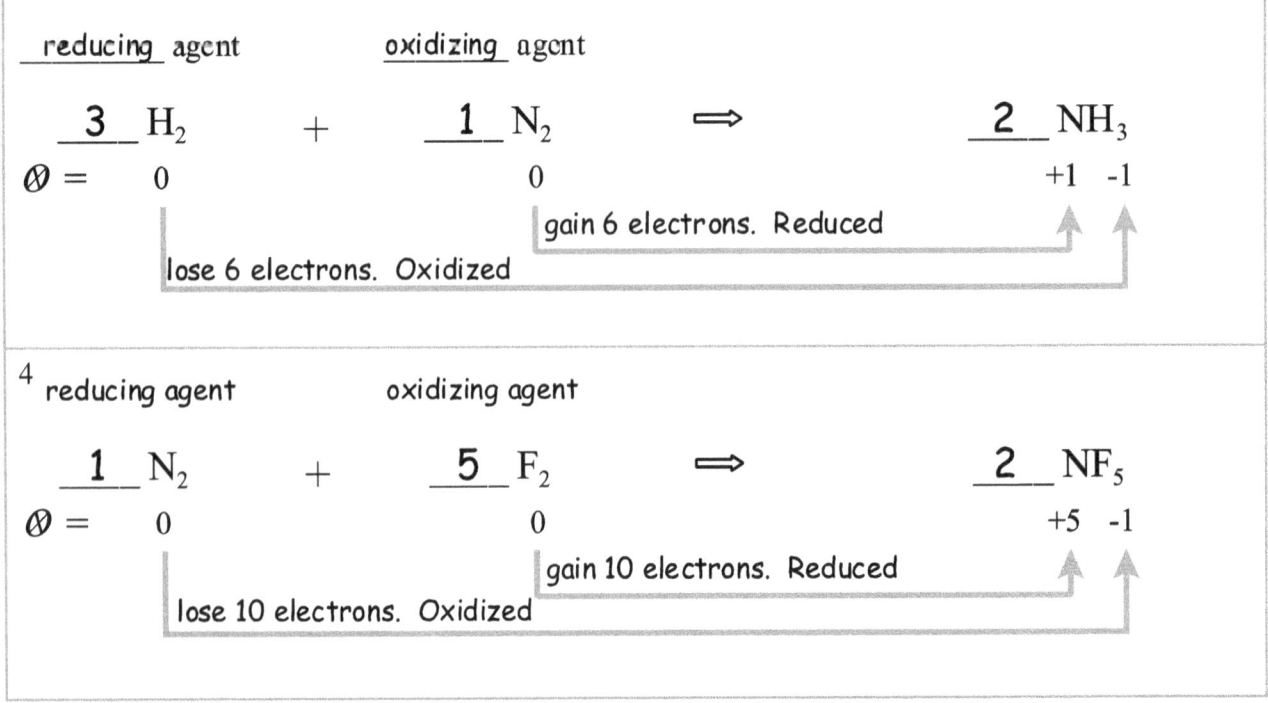

... Between Metals and Non-metals

Ideas About Science and Pedagogy

Try these demonstrations... *in the fume hood!!*

Aluminum and Iodine
Place 1 tsp each of aluminum powder and fine iodine crystals on a sheet of waxed paper. Hold the paper by its edges, and make a trough. Gently roll the two substances back and forth together until they are thoroughly mixed. Do not grind. Put the mixture into a wide crucible in the fume hood, and add one drop of concentrated sulfuric acid.

Prepare a mixture of Sulfur and Zinc powders in the same manner. Ignite it using a propane torch.

Repeat the procedure with Magnesium and Sulfur powders. Caution: very hot and bright. Eye protecrtion needed.

Activity 2.2: Redox Reactions Between Metals and Non-Metals

Pedagogical Issues The redox reactions between metals and non-metals are spectacular! This alone makes them memorable to students. Furthermore, the reactions clearly involve a *transfer of electrons* at every level of representation.

Students can easily identify who gains electrons, and who loses electrons, in the transaction. This makes the task of representing the players in a redox reaction relatively easy.

Science Issues Of course, reactions between metals and non-metals usually result in an ionic bond.

In the case of aluminum and iodine, the iodine takes custody of aluminum's electrons. In the process, iodine does become somewhat larger. As aluminum is stripped of its electrons, on the other hand, it becomes much, much smaller.

The slightly swollen iodine ion and smaller aluminum ion can get much closer together than they could have done as intact covalently bonded atoms! This accounts for both the spectacular energy release, and the production of ionic crystal lattice solids.

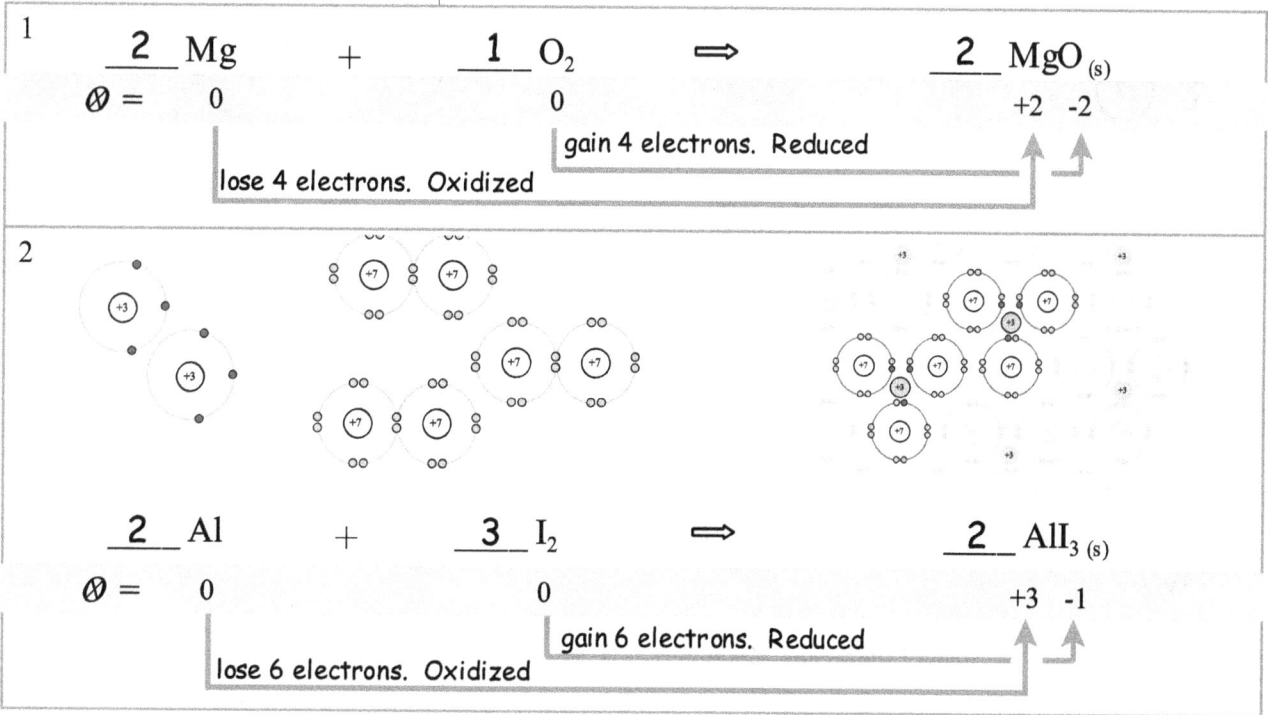

1. __2__ Mg + __1__ O_2 ⟹ __2__ $MgO_{(s)}$

    $\emptyset =$ 0   0   +2 -2

    lose 4 electrons. Oxidized
    gain 4 electrons. Reduced

2. __2__ Al + __3__ I_2 ⟹ __2__ $AlI_{3\ (s)}$

    $\emptyset =$ 0   0   +3 -1

    lose 6 electrons. Oxidized
    gain 6 electrons. Reduced

© Ross Lattner Publishing   www.rosslattner.ca

Redox Reactions ...

Parents and Teachers Guide and Resource

Linus Pauling undertook his ground-breaking work on the chemical bond in the 1930's. He invented the concept of electronegativity to deal with the continuum of bonding models from covalent to ionic.

In the intervening decades, Pauling's concepts have infused the high school syllabus. Unfortunately, his work has been reduced to a "rule:"

when the difference in electronegativity between two elements exceeds 1.7, the chemical bond is ionic.

(Continued....)

Lab 2.3: Redox Reactions Among Non-Metal Elements

Pedagogical Issues It is more difficult for students to perceive redox reactions in non-metals. The principal reason is that neither Lewis dot diagrams nor the oxidation number rules are unequivocally clear about *which* electrons are moving. The second reason is that, properly speaking, oxidation of a non-metal does not involve the *loss* of its electrons. When a non-metal atom is oxidized, its electrons are pulled *away* from the atom in a polar covalent bond, but not entirely lost.

The Ross diagram provides a representation that permits students to identify which electrons are "moving" as the new covalent bonds form. Furthermore, the students can be made aware of the influences that drive the motion of the electrons.

Science Issues Molecular elements, such as chlorine Cl_2, oxygen O_2, have two important features in this discussion. They have an oxidation number of zero, and they have non-polar bonds.

Redox reactions among non-metals *must* change those characteristics. After a redox reaction between non-metal elements, the atoms have *both* a non-zero oxidation number *and* polar covalent bonds. In fact, both of these properties must occur together, as is abundantly clear in the Ross model.

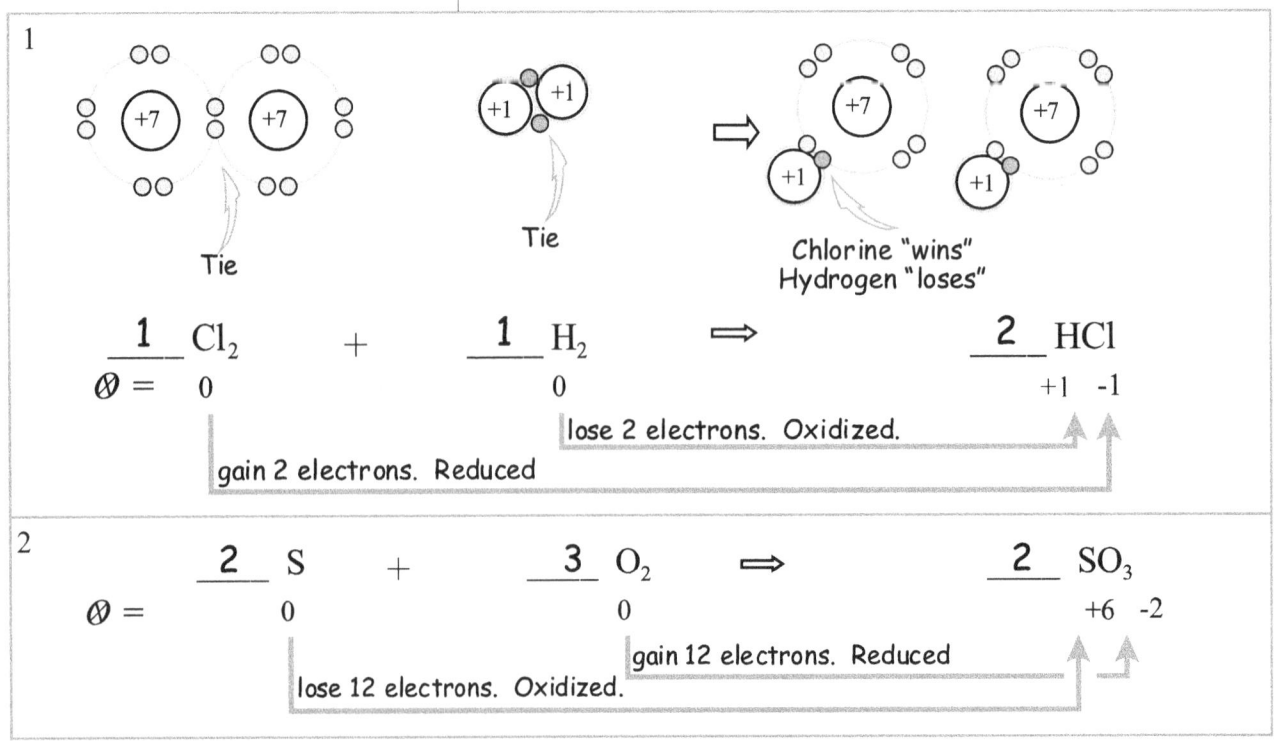

... Among Covalent Molecules

Science and Pedagogy

(....Continued)

For at least three generations, students have memorized the rule, perhaps without comprehending the dynamic behind it.

These reactions are examples of the subtle dynamics of covalent compounds involved in redox reactions.

Lab 2.4: Redox Reactions Among Covalent Molecules

Pedagogical Issues The issues described in Lab 2.3 are much more in evidence here. The questions make no distinctions between electrons. In the answers, the most weakly bound electrons are darkest ●, the most strongly bound electrons are lightest ○, and those in the mid-range are mid-grey ◉. The student can more easily decide which electrons have moved toward or away from each atom.

Science Issues Redox reactions among molecules are subtle. The movement of electrons is not simple. In the second problem in the examples here, we find that no redox reaction has occurred.

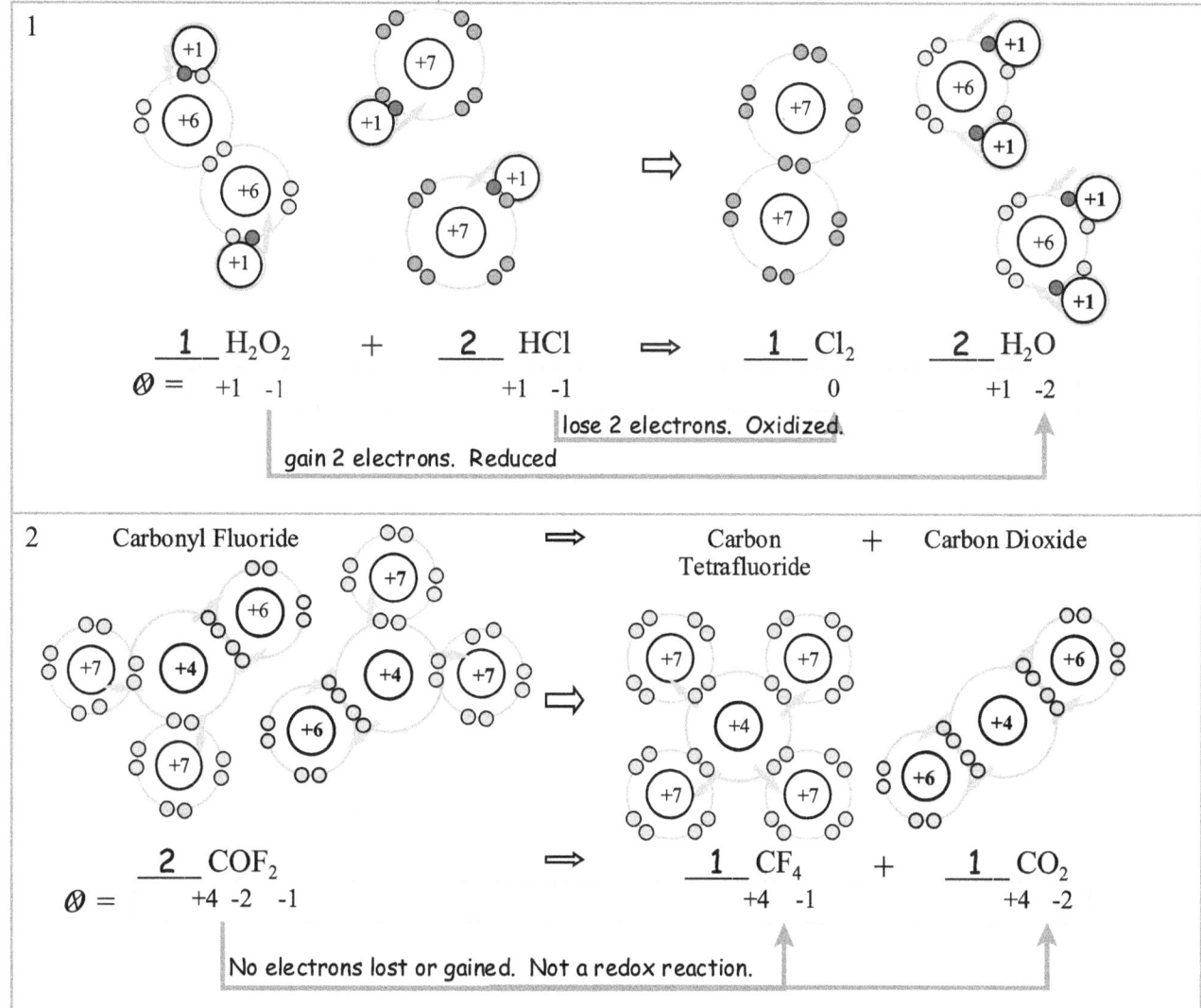

© Ross Lattner Publishing   www.rosslattner.ca

Redox Reactions ...

Parents and Teachers Guide and Resource

Quiz 2: Redox Reactions

It's possible that this reaction is too toxic to be conducted in a secondary school, but interesting nonetheless.

1. Lithium and Oxygen. Before reaction, atoms of lithium and oxygen can get only as close as their radii permit. When oxygen takes custody of lithium's electron, O swells a little, but Li contracts to a very small size. The entire system of ions can get closer in the crystal lattice than they could as neutral atoms.

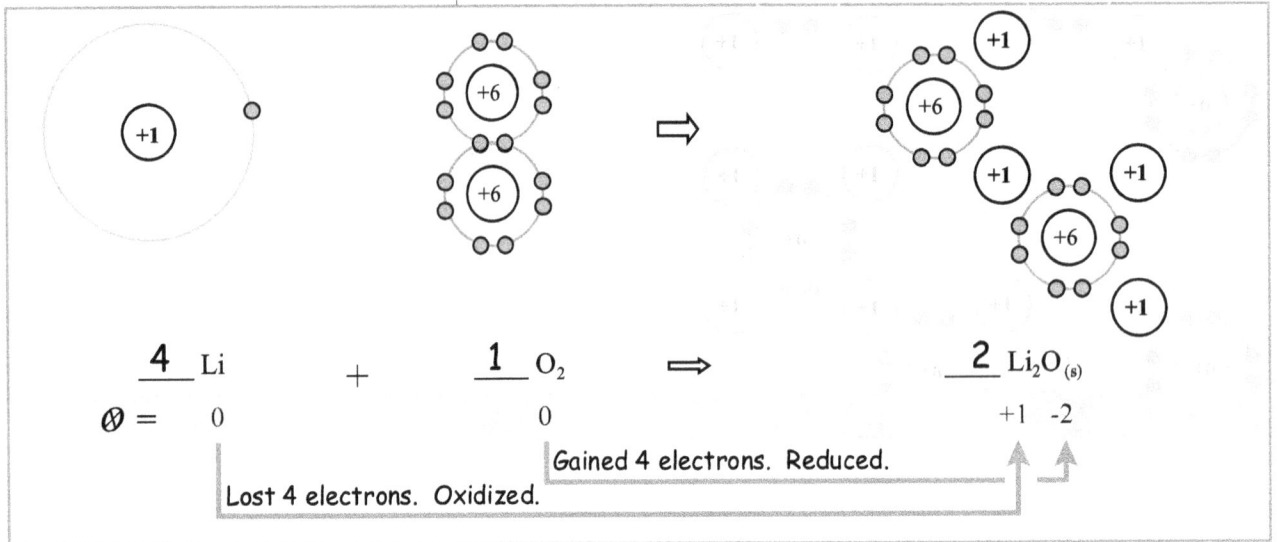

__4__ Li + __1__ O_2 ⇒ __2__ $Li_2O_{(s)}$

∅ =   0   0   +1 −2

Lost 4 electrons. Oxidized.
Gained 4 electrons. Reduced.

Prepare $HI_{(g)}$ by running conc. H_2SO_4 into $KI_{(s)}$ in a gas generator in a fume hood. Trap the HI gas in a flask. Add 2 mL bromine water. Brown I_2 solution will be displaced from HI.

2. Hydrogen iodide and bromine gas. Hydrogen's electrons end up closer to a +7 core charge than they started. All of the other electrons on I and Br stay pretty much the same distance from the +7 core as they started.

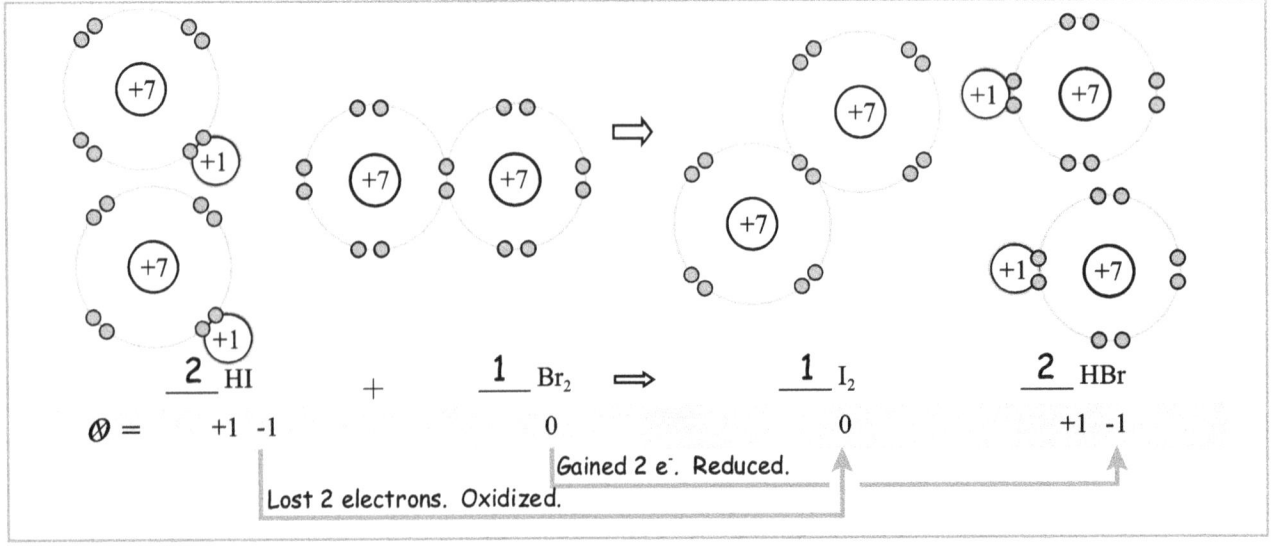

__2__ HI + __1__ Br_2 ⇒ __1__ I_2 + __2__ HBr

∅ =   +1 −1   0   0   +1 −1

Lost 2 electrons. Oxidized.
Gained 2 e⁻. Reduced.

© Ross Lattner Publishing   www.rosslattner.ca

Quiz

Ideas About Science and Pedagogy

Airborne SO_2 can undergo a photochemical reaction with oxygen to produce sulfur trioxide. Dissolved in water, SO_3 becomes H_2SO_4.

3. In the diagram below, sulfur's non-bonding electron pairs have been darkened ● for emphasis. Note that in the SO_3 molecule, *more* of these ● electrons are *closer* to *stronger* core charges than in SO_2.

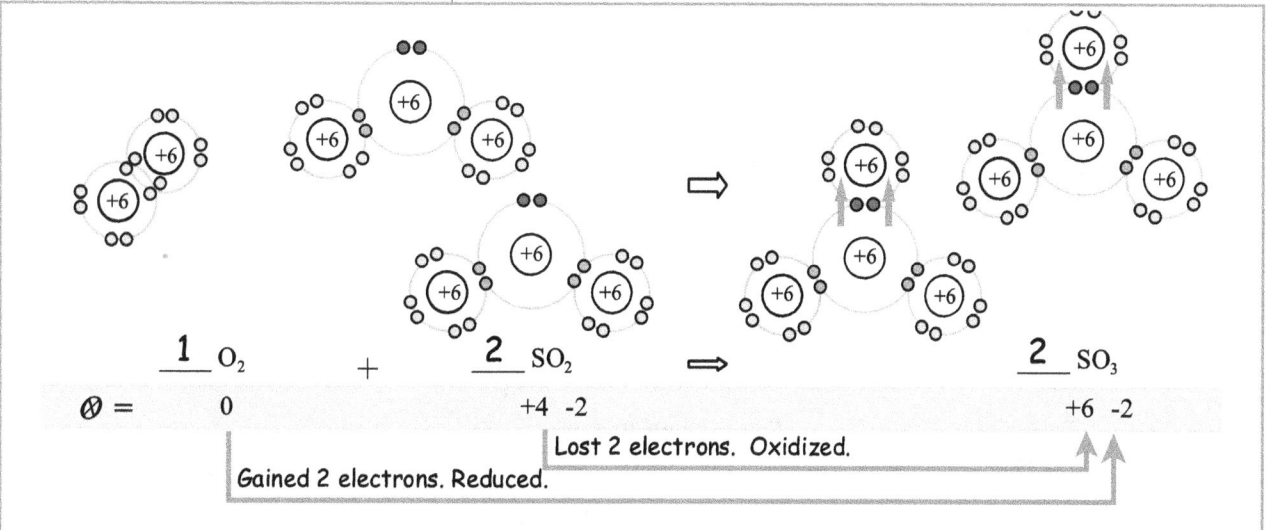

Fill a gas bottle with CO_2 and cover with a glass plate. Light some Mg ribbon in the usual manner, and plunge into the CO_2 gas.

The vigorous reaction produces black carbon! **Caution: do not look directly at the burning Mg !!**

4. There are three atoms here, each with its characteristic χ. Oxygen is strongest, magnesium is weakest and carbon is in the middle. Before the reaction, the strongly held and the medium held electrons are in C=O bonds. The weakly held electrons on Mg are not bonded. After the reaction, the strongest has taken the electrons from the weakest, leaving the medium alone.

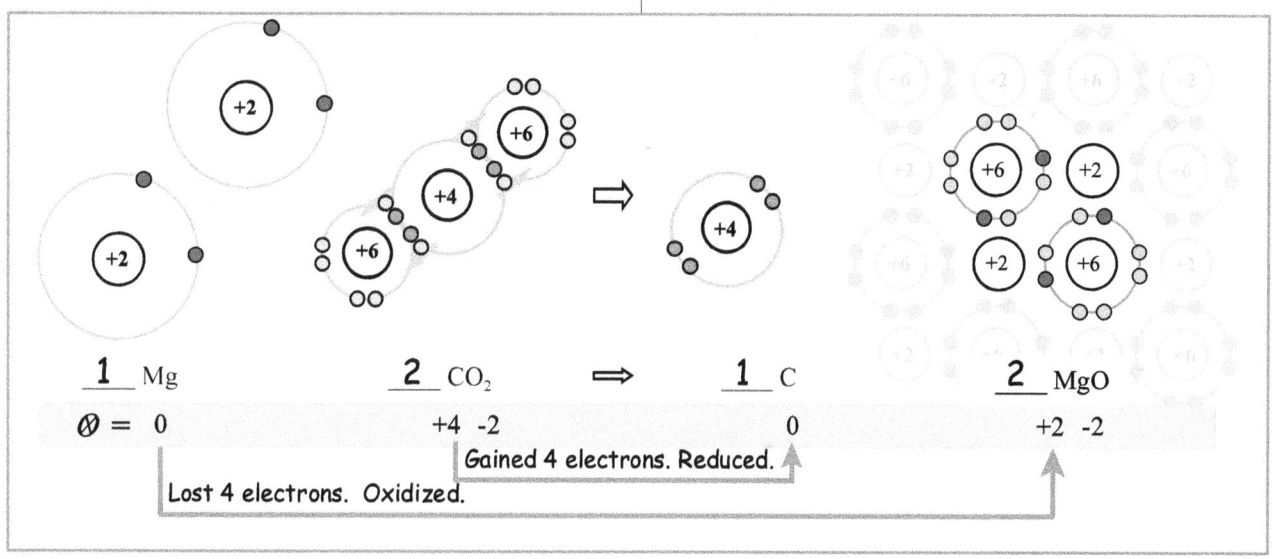

© Ross Lattner Publishing   www.rosslattner.ca

Parents and Teachers Guide and Resource

Redox Reactions ...

The most weakly bound electrons ● are hydrogen's. The most strongly bound electrons ○ belong to oxygen. Those of nitrogen ◐ are in the mid-range and are mid-grey.

5. Once again, we have a situation in which three elements are involved in a reaction. Note that the most weakly bound electrons tend to end up on the most strongly binding atoms, leaving the mid range electrons isolated, or in covalent bonds.

We have seen this pattern in questions 2 and 4 as well. Is this a regular feature of redox reactions?

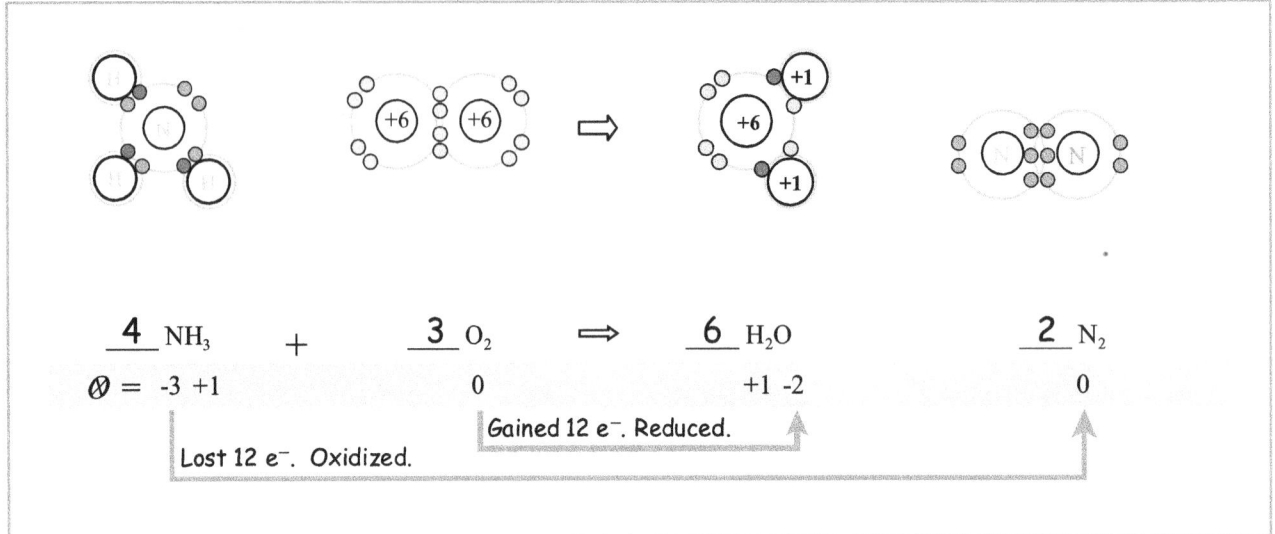

__4__ NH_3 + __3__ O_2 ⇒ __6__ H_2O __2__ N_2

∅ = −3 +1   0   +1 −2   0

Lost 12 e^-. Oxidized.   Gained 12 e^-. Reduced.

The most weakly bound electrons ● are from K. The most strongly bound electrons ○ belong to Cl. Those of Br ◐ are in the mid-range and are mid-grey.

6. The three elements in this redox reaction include one metal, potassium. In the KBr crystal lattice, Br has custody of K's electrons. Bromine, a "middle power," loses custody of potassium's electrons to chlorine, the most strongly attractive atom. This leaves Br isolated.

Is this pattern a regular feature of redox reactions?

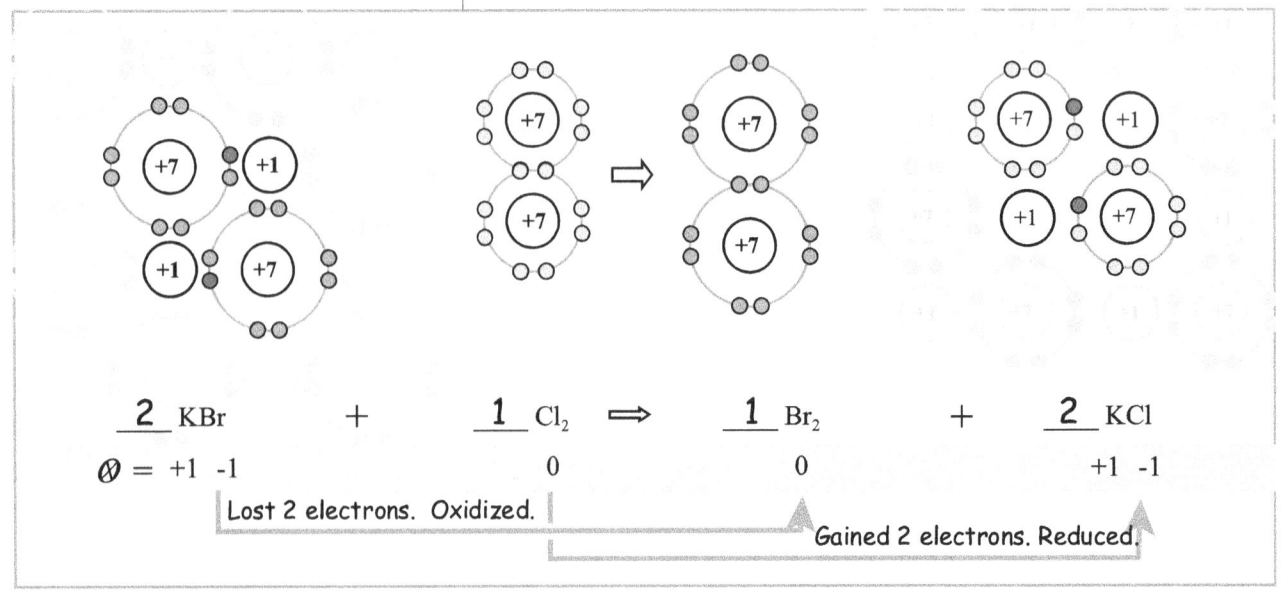

__2__ KBr + __1__ Cl_2 ⇒ __1__ Br_2 + __2__ KCl

∅ = +1 −1   0   0   +1 −1

Lost 2 electrons. Oxidized.   Gained 2 electrons. Reduced.

© Ross Lattner Publishing   www.rosslattner.ca

The most weakly bound electrons ● are hydrogen's. Oxygen's electrons ○ are the most strongly bound. Bromine's ◐ are in the mid-range and are mid-grey.

7. Hydrogen peroxide can liberate free bromine from hydrobromic acid.

Once again, we see the same pattern as in quiz items 2, 4, 5 and 6.

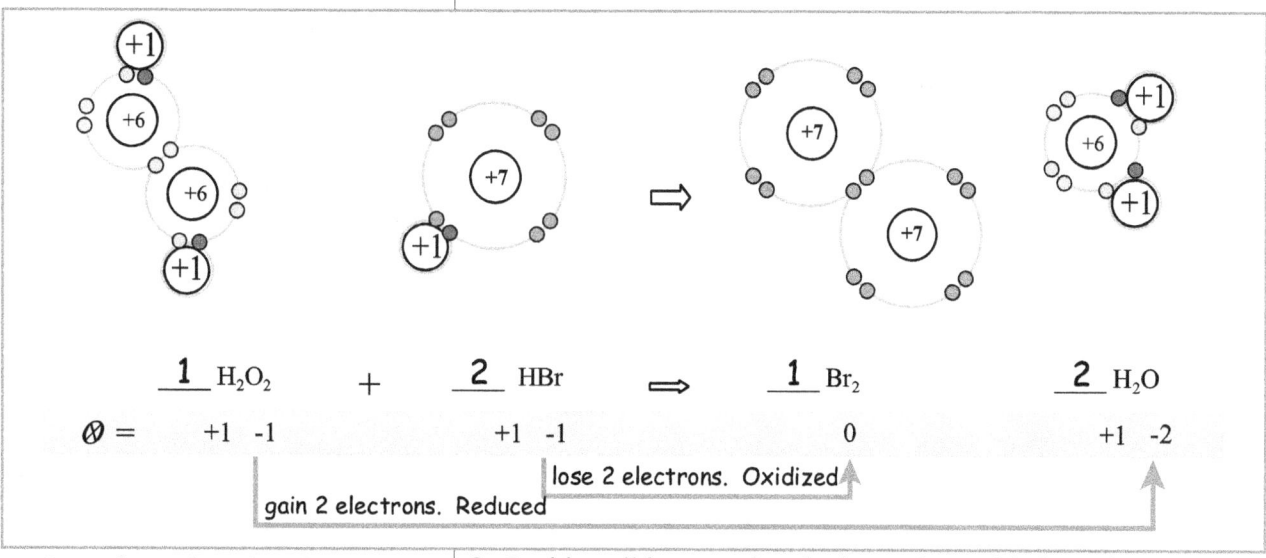

__1__ H$_2$O$_2$ + __2__ HBr ⇒ __1__ Br$_2$ __2__ H$_2$O

∅ =   +1 -1   +1 -1   0   +1 -2

gain 2 electrons. Reduced

lose 2 electrons. Oxidized

In a fume hood... Put 50 mL of household bleach into a 1000 mL graduate. Add 25 mL of conc. HCl. A cloud of Cl$_2$ gas will form in the cylinder. Add sodium sulfite solution to destroy the Cl$_2$.

8. In this striking reaction, hydrogen's weakly bound electrons once again end up in the vicinity of oxygen. Chlorine, the "middle power," is once again left isolated.

From the formal point of view, it looks as if the two chlorines oxidize and reduce each other.

Could it be that oxygen and hydrogen play a critical role in this redox reactions?

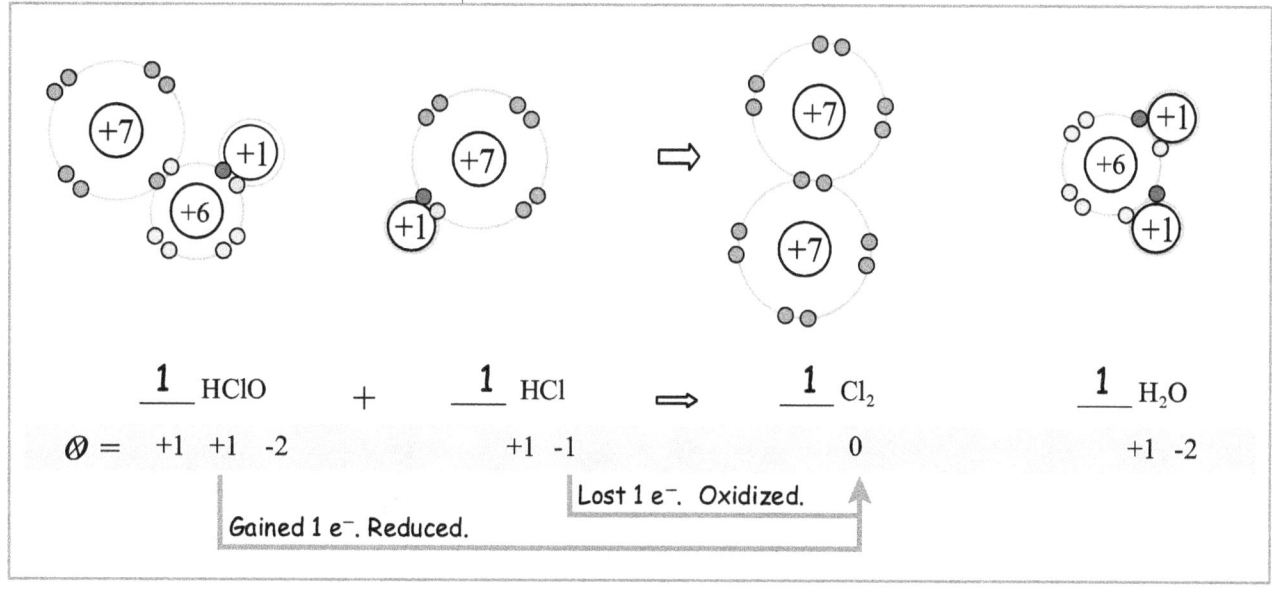

__1__ HClO + __1__ HCl ⇒ __1__ Cl$_2$ __1__ H$_2$O

∅ = +1 +1 -2   +1 -1   0   +1 -2

Gained 1 e⁻. Reduced.

Lost 1 e⁻. Oxidized.

© Ross Lattner Publishing   www.rosslattner.ca

Redox Reactions ...

Parents and Teachers Guide and Resource

Activity 3.1: Carbon and Hydrogen

Among organic chemists, the simplified structural diagram is an indispensable shorthand language. Its power lies in its economy. The scientist who "reads" the language must bring a great deal of knowledge to the spare skeletal diagrams.

Pedagogical Issues The simplified structural diagram is a conceptually dense representational system that can be interpreted in a wide variety of ways. The student's first learning task is back-and-forth translation between the Ross representation system and the simplified structural diagram.

Science Issues The Ross system, layered on top of the traditional simplified structural diagram, provides an expanded set of concepts that enable students to interpret some very important features of organic molecules.

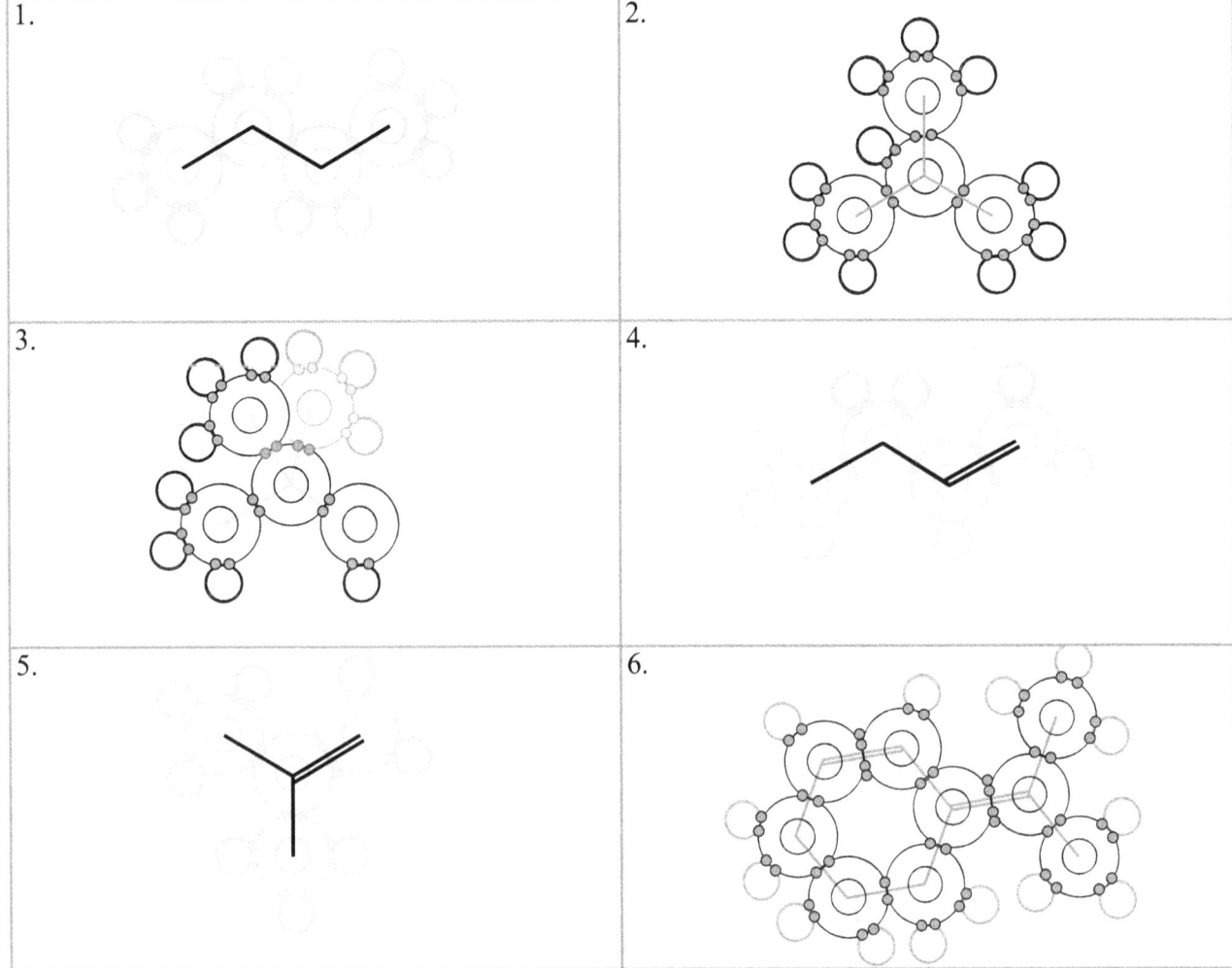

© Ross Lattner Publishing   18   www.rosslattner.ca

... in Organic Chemistry

Ideas About Science and Pedagogy

Activity 3.2: Oxidation Numbers in Hydrocarbons

The traditional oxidation states assigned to carbon include +4 and –4. These tend to refer to "special cases" of organic chemistry, such as CO_2 and CH_4. Otherwise, they apply more generally to the inorganic chemistry of carbon, such as CF_4.

Pedagogical Issues Within organic molecules, carbon can display all oxidation states between +3 and –3. The oxidation chemistry of carbon within organic molecules is thus much more complex than traditional high school curricula can cover. With the Ross system layered on top of the traditional simplified structural diagram, students can quickly and easily identify carbon's oxidation states.

Science Issues In both the disciplines of synthetic organic chemistry and in biochemistry, the ability to follow subtle changes in oxidation state is an important skill for science students and practitioners.

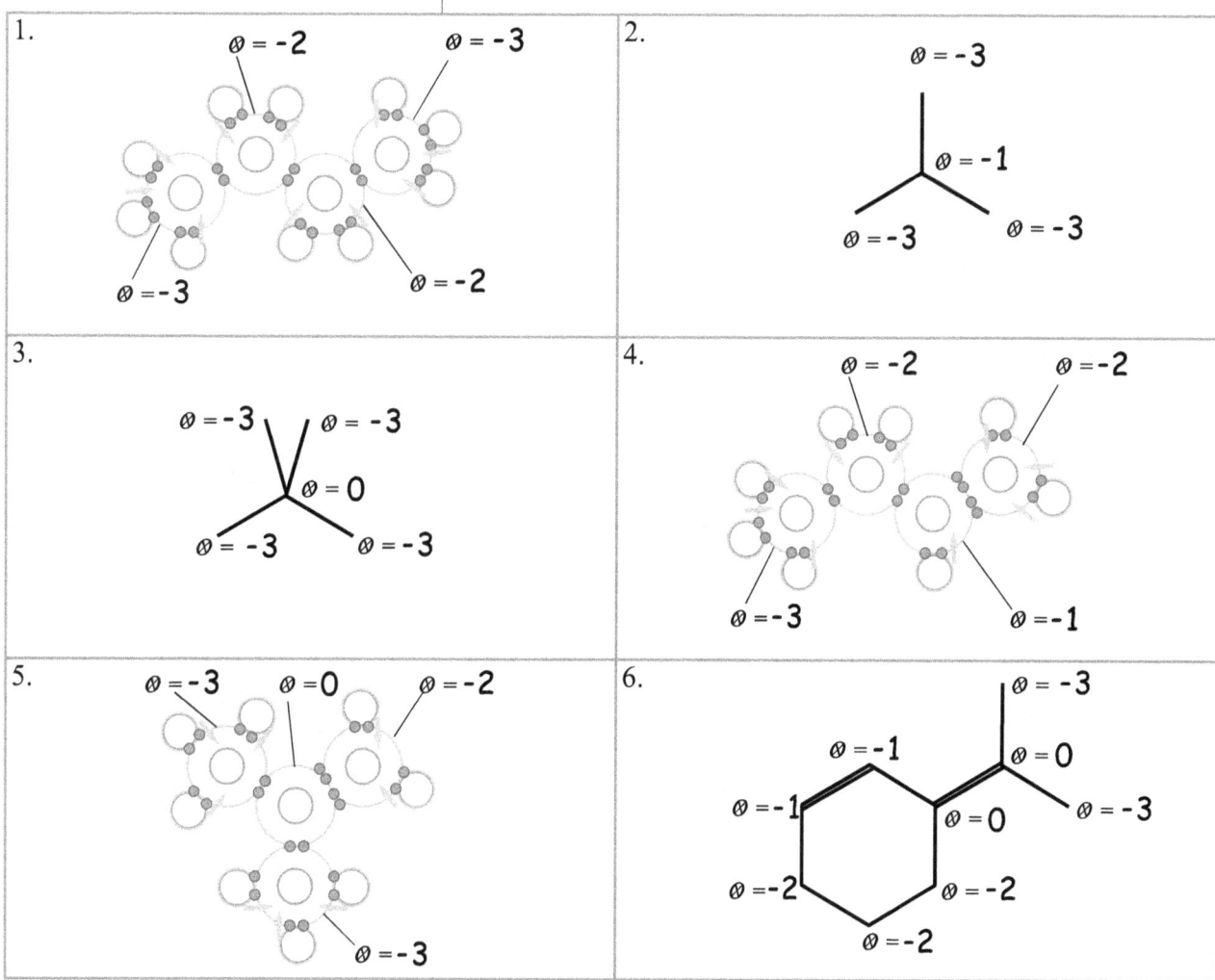

© Ross Lattner Publishing   19   www.rosslattner.ca

Parents and Teachers Guide and Resource

Redox Reactions ...

In any field of study, beginners find it difficult to think in terms of systems. Beginning learners tend to seize upon the large features of the new object of study, and to ascribe fixed roles to those features. Students, for example, want to know "what a carbonyl group does." Experts have learned to see the carbonyl group as a "system of inter-related parts."

Activity 3.3: Oxygen and Nitrogen in Organic Molecules

Pedagogical Issues The functionality of oxygen containing groups in organic molecules is complex. Functionality depends not upon the gross structure of the carbonyl group, for example, but on the possible interactions of the carbon and oxygen with other features on the molecule and in the environment. We want our students to begin to perceive how the parts of each functional group contribute to the whole.

Science Issues The core charge and radius of oxygen and nitrogen influence the behavior of carbon's electrons. Possibly the simplest influence for a beginner to perceive is oxidation state. The skill set to calculate oxidation number is the same as in Activity 3.2.

1.
∅ = −2, ∅ = −2

2.
∅ = −2 (O)
∅ = +2
∅ = −3, ∅ = −3

3. The carboxyl carbon is oxidized to +3.
∅ = −3
∅ = −2
∅ = +3
∅ = −2
∅ = −3   ∅ = −2 OH
∅ = +3
O ∅ = −2

4.
∅ = −2 (O)
∅ = −1, ∅ = −1
∅ = −3, ∅ = −3

5.
O ∅ = −2
∅ = +3   ∅ = −2
∅ = −3 NH$_2$
HO
∅ = −2   ∅ = 0   ∅ = +3
NH$_2$ O ∅ = −2
∅ = −3

6.
∅ = −2
H O
∅ = 0
∅ = −1   ∅ = −1
H O   H O
∅ = −2   ∅ = −2

... in Organic Chemistry

Ideas About Science and Pedagogy

Activity 3.4: Redox Reactions of Organic Molecules

Schools of pedagogical thought often differ over the relative prominence of acquiring skills and acquiring conceptual understanding. In practice, skills and concepts interplay with each other.

Pedagogical Issues The "half-cell method" for balancing redox reactions is a skill set that the student uses to sharpen up his or her grasp of the concepts of redox reactions. The skills comprising the "half-cell method" are not as useful for probing the details of redox reactions in organic chemistry. The Ross approach may provide an alternative skill set, so that beginning students can investigate redox reactions in carbon compounds.

Science Issues These reactions are commonly undertaken in high school labs to investigate differences in 1°, 2° and 3° alcohols.

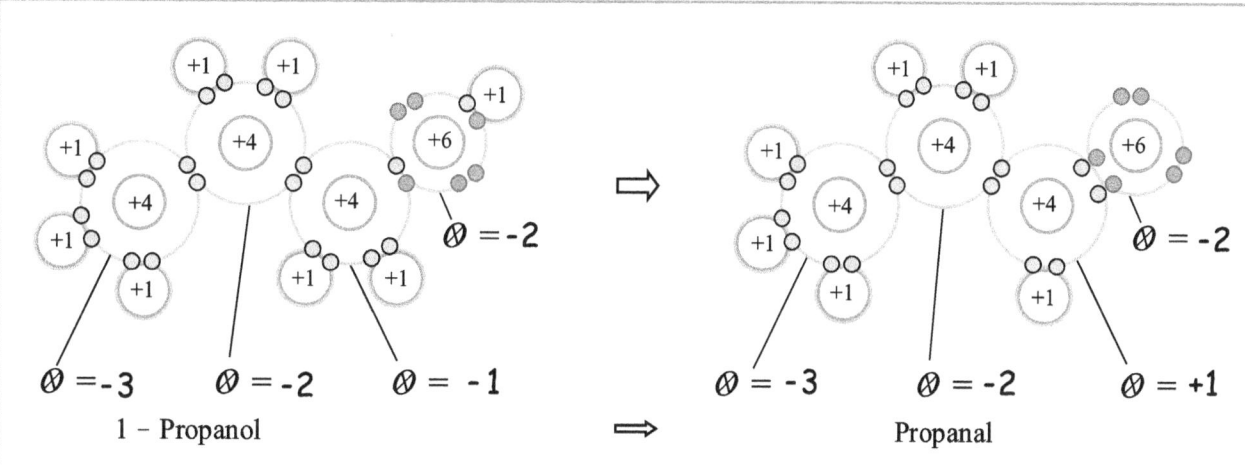

1 - Propanol ⟹ Propanal

$$10\ H^+ + 3\ CH_3CH_2CH_2OH + 2\ CrO_4^{2-} \Longrightarrow 3\ CH_3CH_2CHO + 2\ Cr^{3+} + 8\ H_2O$$

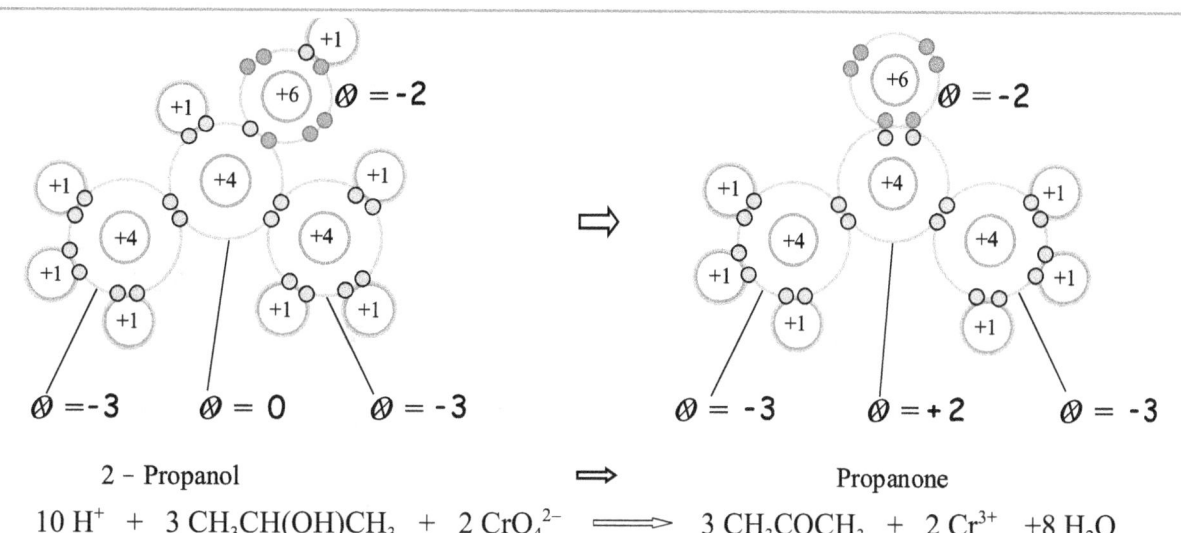

2 - Propanol ⟹ Propanone

$$10\ H^+ + 3\ CH_3CH(OH)CH_3 + 2\ CrO_4^{2-} \Longrightarrow 3\ CH_3COCH_3 + 2\ Cr^{3+} + 8\ H_2O$$

© Ross Lattner Publishing   www.rosslattner.ca

Parents and Teachers Guide and Resource

Redox Reactions ...

Quiz 3: Oxidation and Reduction in Organic Chemistry

1.
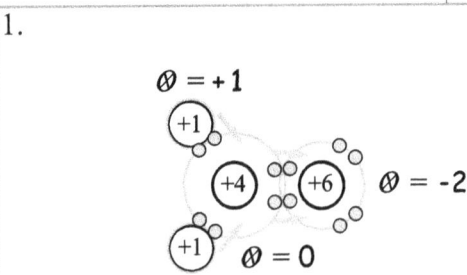

2.
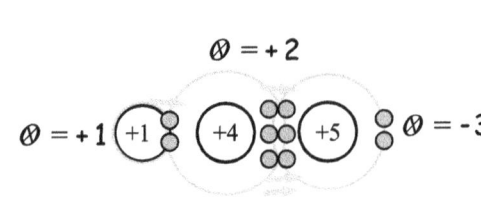

3.
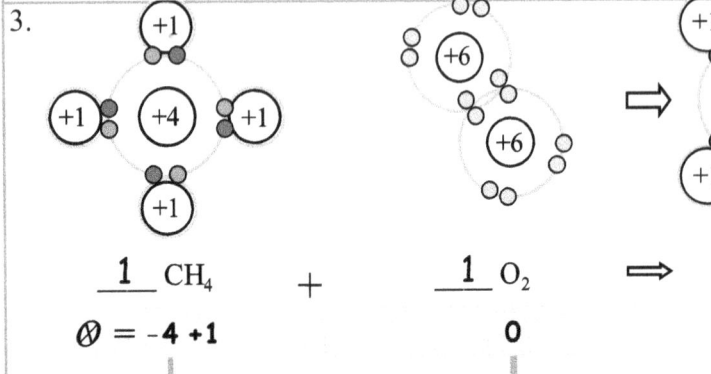

___1___ CH_4 + ___1___ O_2 ⇒ ___1___ H_2CO ___1___ H_2O

Ø = −4 +1   0   +1 0 −2   +1 −2

Lost 4 electrons oxidized   Gain 4 electrons reduced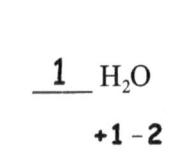

4.
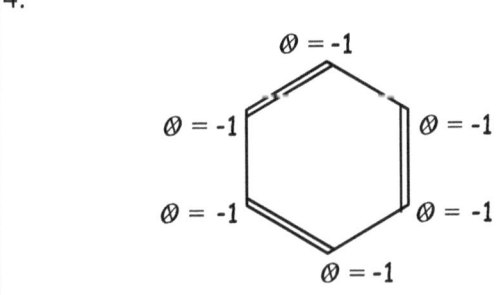

5.
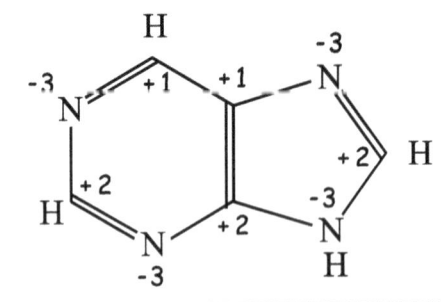

6.
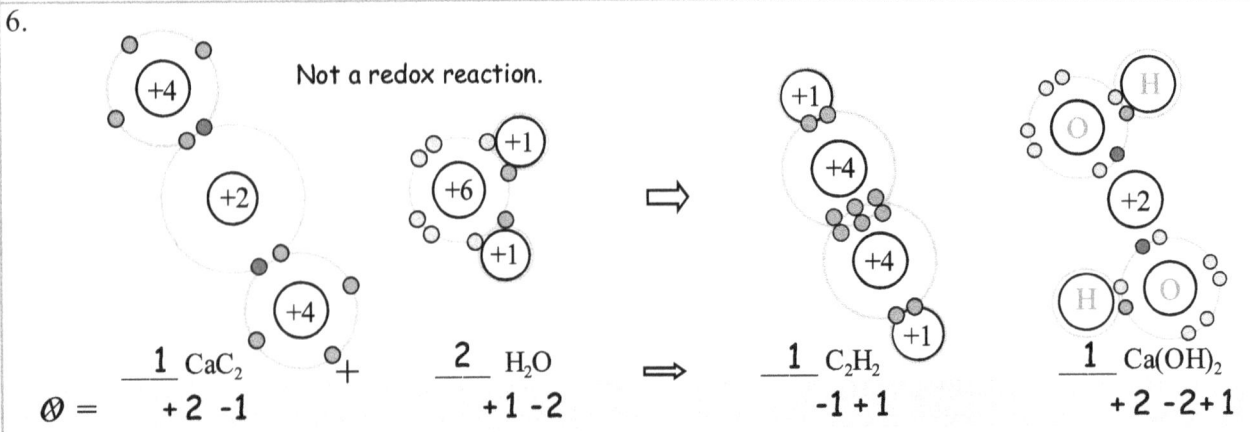

Not a redox reaction.

___1___ CaC_2 + ___2___ H_2O ⇒ ___1___ C_2H_2 ___1___ $Ca(OH)_2$

Ø =   +2 −1   +1 −2   −1 +1   +2 −2 +1

© Ross Lattner Publishing   www.rosslattner.ca

... in Organic Chemistry

Ideas About Science and Pedagogy

Quiz 3: Oxidation and Reduction in Organic Chemistry

7.
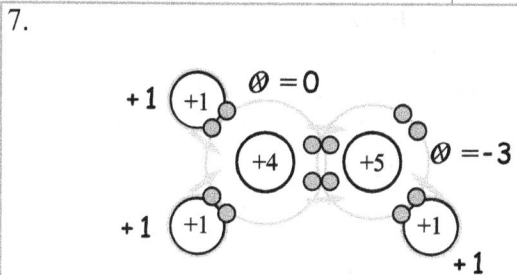

8.
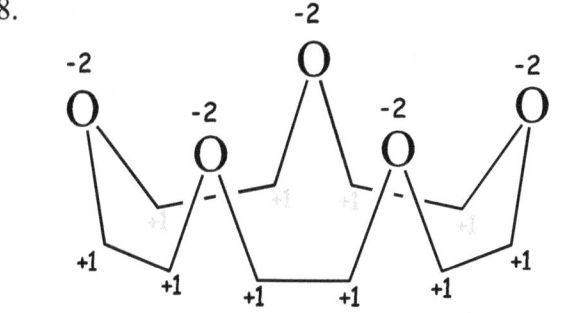

9.
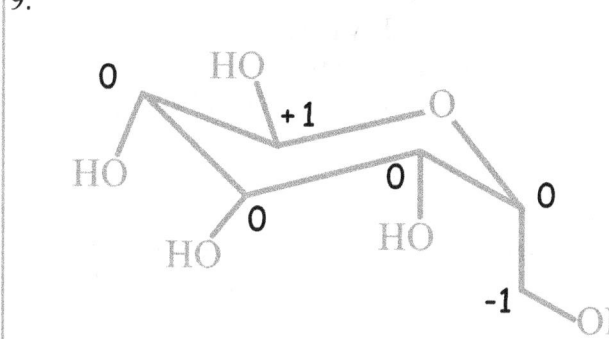

The six carbons end up with an oxidation number of 0, +1, or −1. The average is zero.

Since all of the carbon came from carbon (+4) dioxide, each carbon has gained four electrons on the average.

Note that glucose, the fuel that runs our planet, contains carbon with the same average oxidation state as elemental carbon.

10.
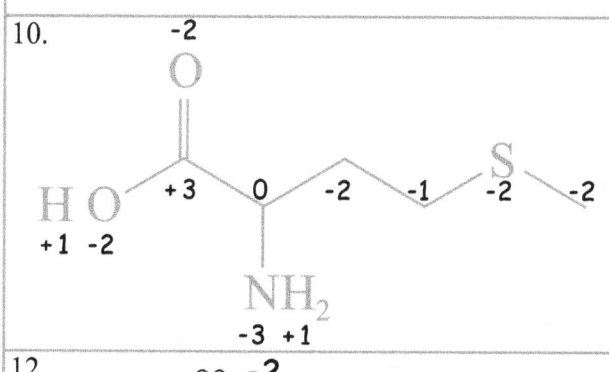

11.
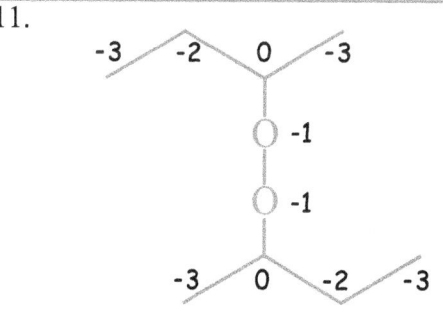

12.
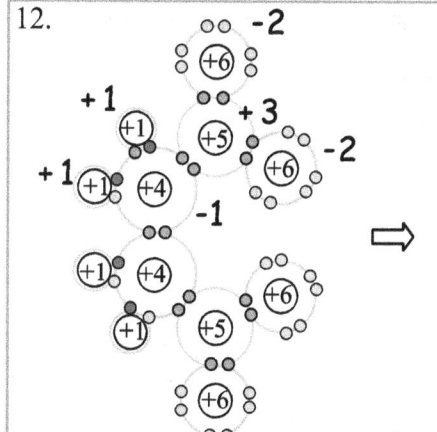 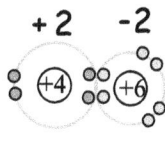 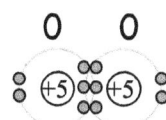 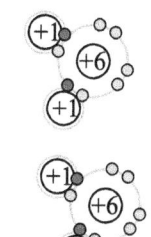

Two carbons lose 3 electrons each
Two nitrogens gain 3 electrons each
This is a redox reaction.

© Ross Lattner Publishing   www.rosslattner.ca

Parents and Teachers Guide and Resource

Electrons and Energy ...

The Ross table is designed for learners. With representations of core charge and radius, students can make use of their schematic thinking to make scientifically sound judgements about the behavior of atoms and molecules.

Unfortunately, of all of the schematic reasoning structures that students use to make sense of their world, none correspond to the scientist's concept of energy.

This may account for some of the conceptual difficulties that students appear to have when they first encounter the energy concept - and why the energy concept appeared so late in history.

Activity 4.1: Electron Potential Energy

Pedagogical Issues Up to this point, students have been using the *Effort schema* to make predictions about the effect of core charge upon electron behavior, and the *Proximity schema* to predict the effect of radius. If we are going to introduce the concept of energy, we need to support the student as he or she steps away from using schematic reasoning to a more accurate understanding of energy.

Science Issues The concept of a "potential energy well" is widely understood among scientists as depicting a relationship between the potential energy and the position of an object.

If we use the potential well as a sideways view of the Ross model, the student can alternate between a familiar "face on" understanding of the Ross and the "sideways" view of a potential well.

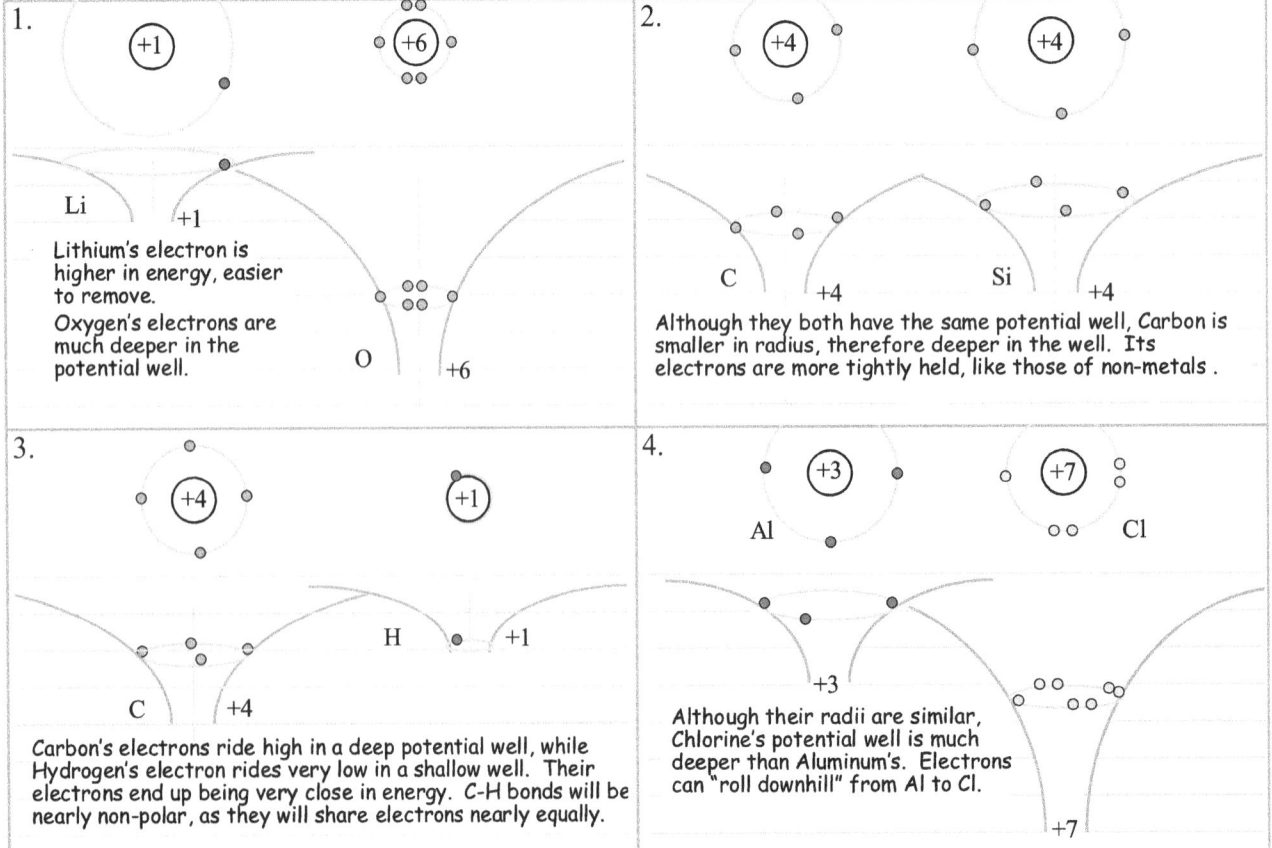

1. Li +1
Lithium's electron is higher in energy, easier to remove.
Oxygen's electrons are much deeper in the potential well.
O +6

2. C +4   Si +4
Although they both have the same potential well, Carbon is smaller in radius, therefore deeper in the well. Its electrons are more tightly held, like those of non-metals.

3. C +4
Carbon's electrons ride high in a deep potential well, while Hydrogen's electron rides very low in a shallow well. Their electrons end up being very close in energy. C-H bonds will be nearly non-polar, as they will share electrons nearly equally.

4. Al +3   Cl +7
Although their radii are similar, Chlorine's potential well is much deeper than Aluminum's. Electrons can "roll downhill" from Al to Cl.

... "Falling" Toward the Core

Ideas About Science and Pedagogy

Every act of "teaching" falls short. Every teacher must choose among competing poverties of explanation. We can only choose the *nature* of the insufficiency.

Should we avoid the question?

accept misleading simplicities?

or be merely incomplete?

Activity 4.2: The Combustion of Non-Metals

Pedagogical Issues The subject of chemical bonding is complex. The picture presented here is admittedly inadequate. In its defense, we point out that it is not misleading, or wrong, but incomplete. There is much more to be said about the interaction between electric potential fields and the electrons that populate them. Nevertheless, this picture provides the student with a beginner's grasp of "higher" and "lower" potential energies, and the tendencies of electrons as they respond to this potential energy environment.

Science Issues The energy of chemical bonds and chemical reactions is more complex than the depiction here can provide. Nevertheless, the idea that core charge and valence radius affect electron potential energy in a predictable way is a new and valuable concept for the beginning chemistry student. The picture is not wrong in the details selected, just incomplete.

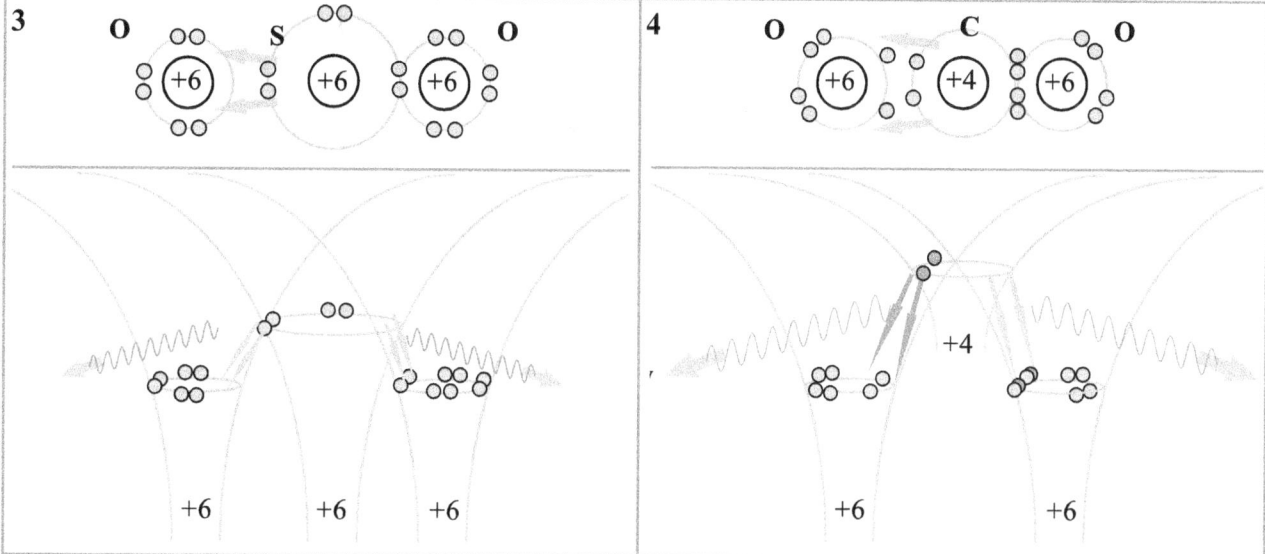

5 Oxygen and sulfur both have a +6 core charge, therefore they both have the same deep potential well. Because oxygen's radius is smaller than sulfur's, its electrons are farther down in the potential well than sulfur's.

Carbon's +4 core charge provides a shallower potential well. Because carbon's radius is larger than oxygen's, its valence electrons are higher still in potential energy, even higher than sulfur's.

Carbon's electrons fall farther than sulfur's as they plunge into oxygen's potential well. Burning carbon, therefore, will release more energy than burning sulfur.

Parents and Teachers Guide and Resource

Electrons and Energy ...

The Born-Haber thermochemical account of the energy of formation of ionic solids:

1. Break elements into atoms

2. Remove electrons from gaseous metal atoms, and add them to non-metal atoms

3. Coalesce ions into crystals

1 + 2 + 3 together equal:

4. Elements → Ionic Crystal

Activity 4.3: The Spectacular Combustion of Metals

Pedagogical Issues Looking "down the throat" of the Ross model of atoms, metals have "weak" core charges and large radii. Seen "from the side," this corresponds to electrons riding very high on the outer rim of a shallow potential well. Non-metals have strong core charges and deep potential wells. The electrons ride very far down the well on a small radius.

Science Issues The traditional approach to the energy of the combustion of metals has involved a dissection of the reaction into four distinct thermochemical processes, linked into a Born-Haber cycle. This approach concludes that the greatest portion of the overall energy of formation of an ionic solid is due to crystal lattice energy, that is, the energy released when ions attract and coalesce into crystals.

The Ross approach dissects the combustion of magnesium into just two processes: (1) the movement of electrons from higher to lower potential energy, and (2) the movement of the resulting ions into a denser packing of charges than before ionization.

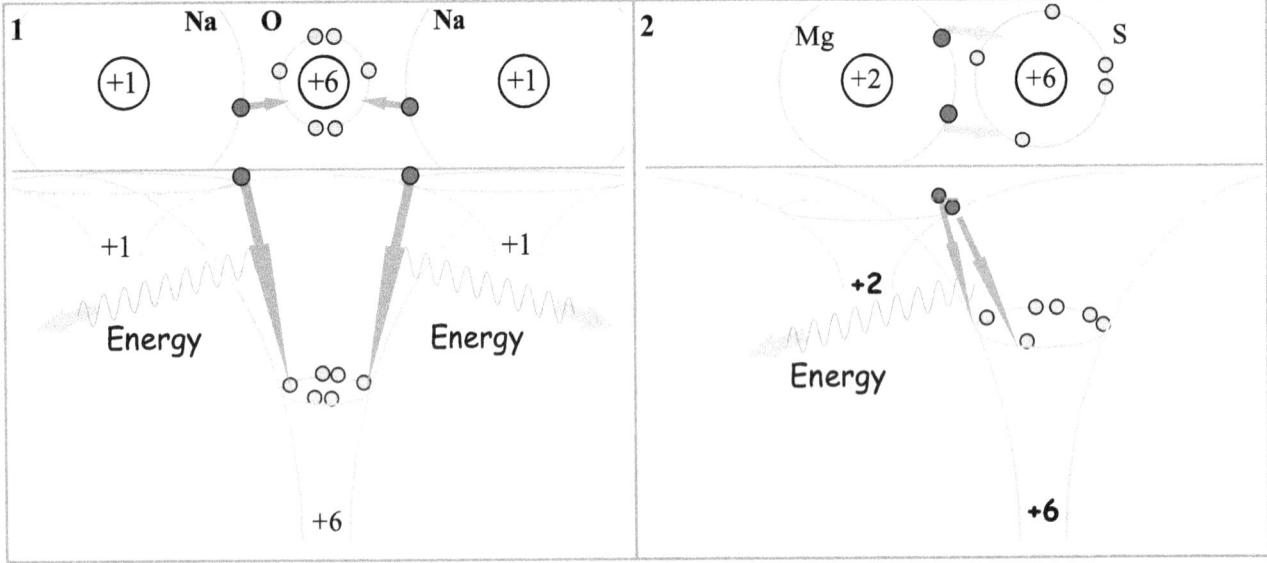

3. In the first process, as magnesium's electrons fall into the custody of oxygen's greater core charge and smaller radius, their potential energy is transformed into heat. Magnesium's electrons would fall further down into oxygen than they would into sulfur, releasing more heat.

In the second process, oxygen's ions would be smaller than sulfur's, so the MgO crystal lattice would be more tightly packed than the MgS lattice. The formation of MgO would release more heat.

... "Falling" Toward the Core

Ideas About Science and Pedagogy

When beginning students are confronted with the difference in the reactions of acetylene and methane with air, they are likely to attempt to explain the difference by speaking of acetylene being "stronger" or "weaker" than methane.

Activity 4.4: The Combustion of Methane

Pedagogical Issues Our task is to encourage the students to attend to all of the forces involved, and to use the terms "stronger" and "weaker" where they are most scientifically applicable.

Science Issues The electrons that are highest in energy ● belong to hydrogen and carbon. Oxygen's electrons ○ are the most strongly bound.

1, 2 The C-H covalent bonds in acetylene are formed when electrons are attracted into the space between a +1 *and* +4 core charge. In the C-C bond, electrons are attracted into the space between two +4 core charges. See Activity 5.3 for a discussion of the difference between σ and π bonds.

Because of oxygen's small radius and large core charge, the electrons are attracted *out of* their previous arrangement, and *into* a new arrangement in which they are closer to a +6 core charge.

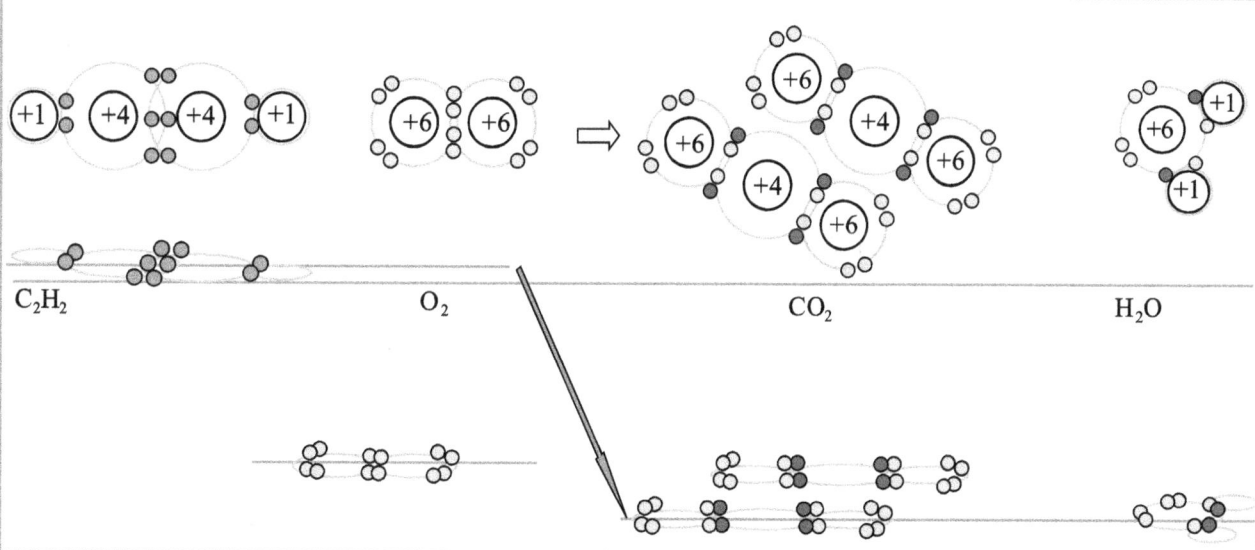

3, 4 The average potential energy of acetylene's electrons is higher than the reference line. The potential energy wells have been left out of this diagram, but acetylene's electrons are higher up in the well than they would have been even in the pure elements.

3 Burning one molecule of methane would permit 8 electrons to fall to the level of CO_2 and H_2O. Burning one molecule of acetylene would permit 10 electrons to fall from an even higher initial energy level down to the same products. Overall, burning acetylene will release more potential energy than burning methane.

Quiz 4: Electrons and Energy

1.

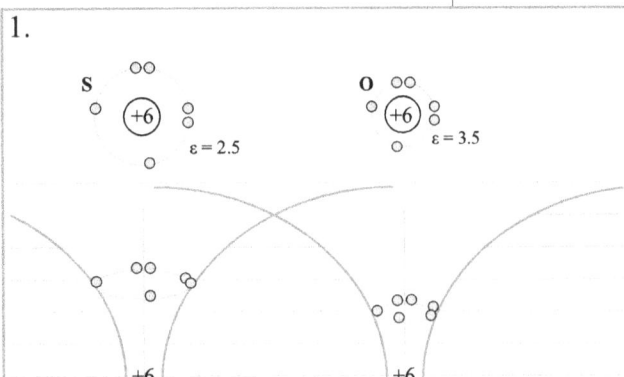

The potential wells are the same. Oxygen's electrons are more tightly attracted, and occupy a smaller radius. Therefore oxygen's valence electrons are lower in potential energy.

2.

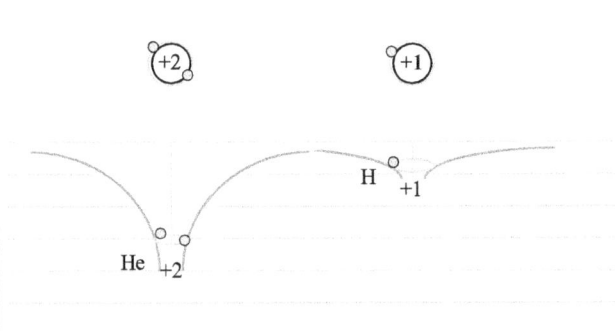

Helium's potential well is deeper than hydrogen's, owing to its greater core charge. Hydrogen's electron is easily removed by any non-metal. Helium's electrons are so deep in the well, that its electrons cannot be removed by any other element.

3.

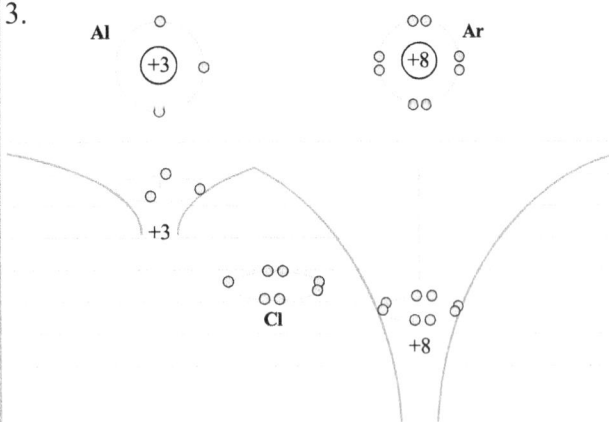

Both elements have the same radius Argon has a greater core charge, therefor its electrons reside in a deeper potential well. Aluminum's smaller core charge results in a much shallower potential well.

Chlorine could pull aluminum's valence electrons down into its lower energy level, but could not induce argon's electrons to "roll uphill."
Aluminum is chemically active, but argon is not.

4.

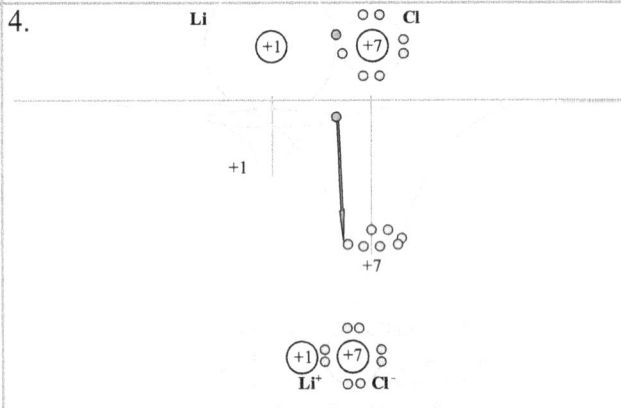

Lithium's loosely held (high energy) valence electron readily drops into chlorine's deep potential well. Chlorine thus "gains custody" of lithium's electron, and Li shrinks to the size of its core.

Energy is released both as the electron falls into the lower energy state *and* as the resulting ions coalesce into an ionic crystal lattice.

Quiz 4: Electrons and Energy

5.

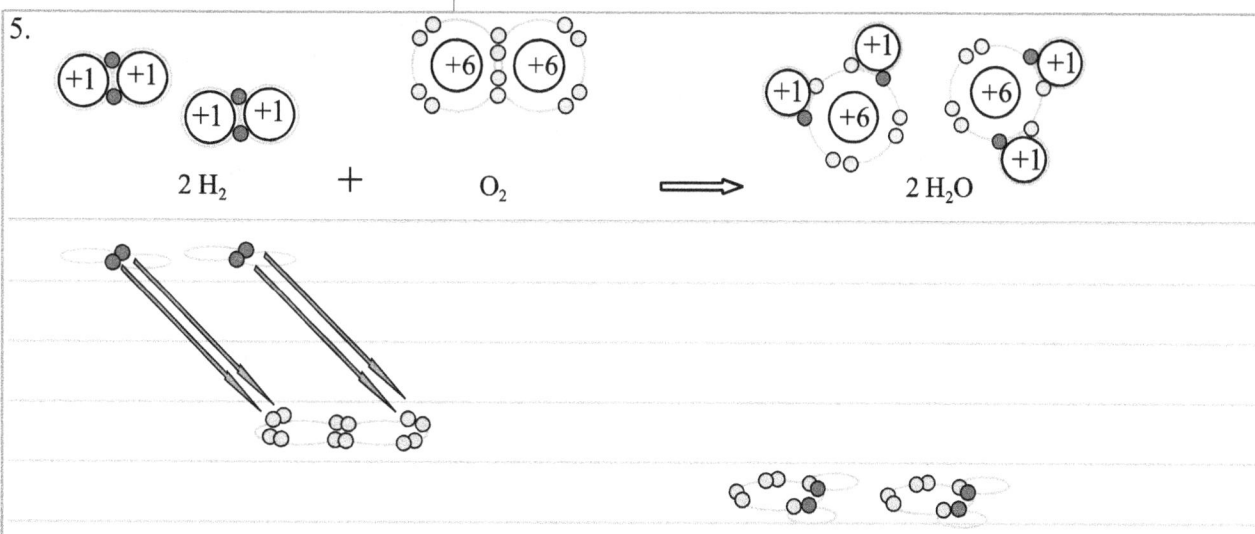

From the Ross perspective, looking "down the funnel" of the potential energy well, hydrogen's electrons would tend to move to a place where they could be close to both a +1 and a +6 core charge. Seen "from the side," hydrogen's electrons fall into oxygen's much deeper potential well. In the space shuttle's main rocket motors, hydrogen's electrons "roll downhill" to oxygen to provide the energy to lift the shuttle into orbit.

6.

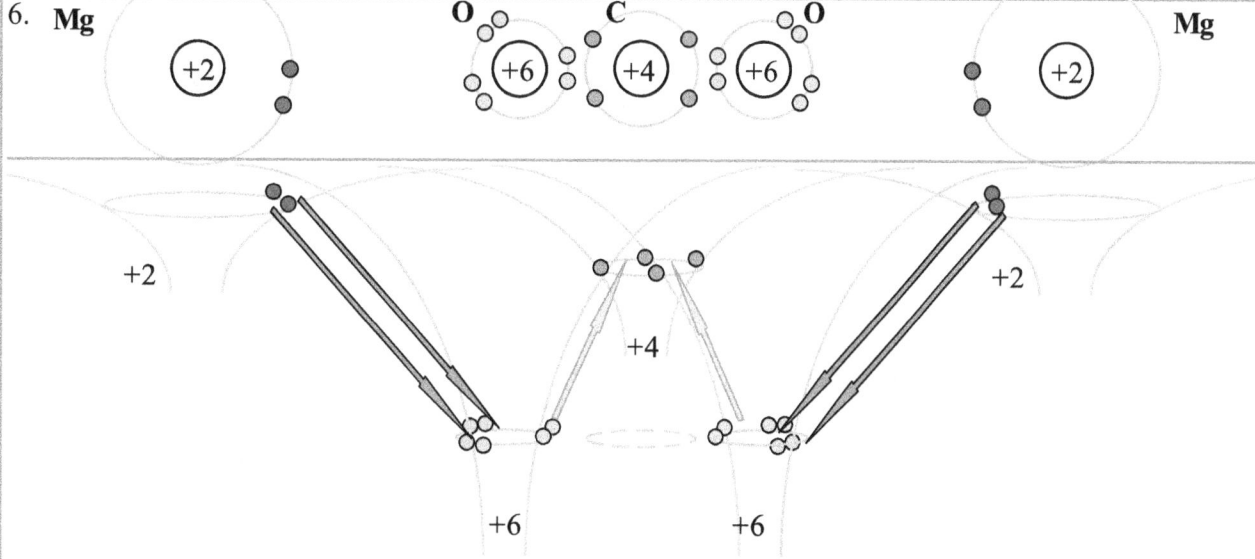

Oxygen's valence electrons are low in energy. Magnesium's electrons are high in energy. If Mg's electrons fell all the way down into oxygen's valence, they could release more than enough energy to lift carbon's electrons back up to the element's original state. Once again, the most weakly bound electrons are attracted into the strongest bound state, pushing the mid-strength electrons without chemical bonds. See Quiz 3 for more examples.

Polar Bonds ...

Parents and Teachers Guide and Resource

Lab 5.1: The Strange Dipolarity of Water

Water is such a remarkable substance! It is the smallest, lightest molecule in our everyday environment. For that reason, it is also the fastest, rattling around in your drinking glass at about 500 m/s. It has a complex structure, including its very large dipole moment. A consequence of all of these properties is the highest specific heat capacity of any common molecule.

Pedagogical Issues Integrating the various factors that affect water's behavior is a non-trivial learning task. While it is unlikely that a student would easily put together such details as water's small mass and its large specific heat capacity, such connections should be made often by the teacher. At the very least, the student who has heard these things and spent a few seconds wondering about the connection is in a better position, months or years later, of making the connection explicit.

Science Issues Water's intense dipole character contributes to its remarkably high melting and boiling points, and its large latent heats of fusion and of vaporization. The small mass and large velocity of water molecules contributes to water's ability to dissolve so many substances, including the nearly insoluble oxygen gas.

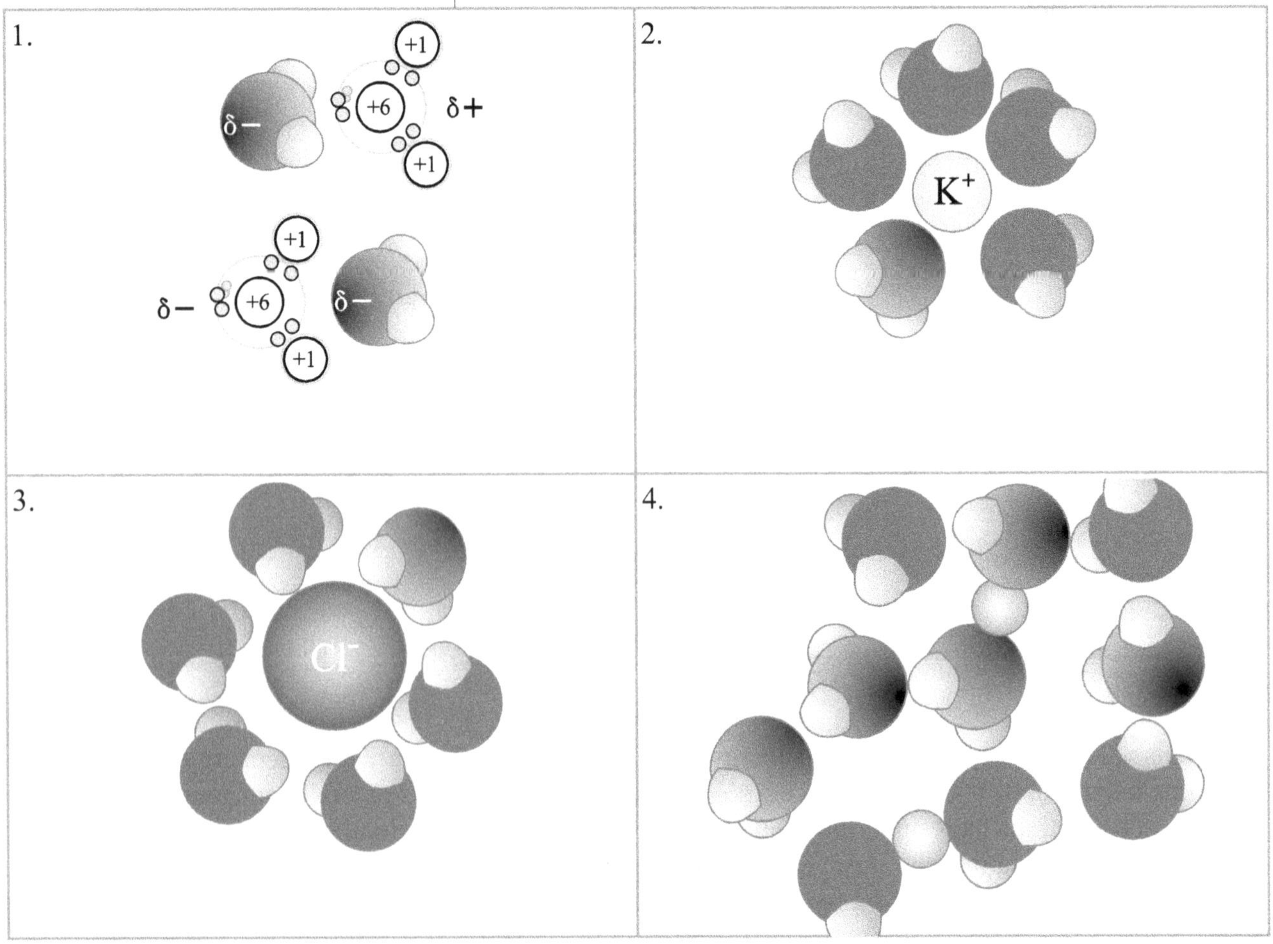

... and Dipole Molecules

Ideas About Science and Pedagogy

Color density is a cognitive stand-in for *electron density*.

In the previous Ross Lattner book **Table Manners** we asked students to "draw" the path of an electron as it meandered around the atomic cores as covalently bonded pairs.

You may wish to refer to that exercise to reinforce the idea of electron density.

Lab 5.2: Alcohols as Dipoles

Pedagogical Issues A picture is worth a thousand words. How can students draw a picture of polarity? Color, or shading, can help students represent electron charge density distributions in molecules.

Science Issues Oxygen's large core charge and small radius provides a strong attraction for electrons in its valence. This is reflected in oxygen's electronegativity $\chi = 3.5$, compared to hydrogen's $\chi = 2.1$.

Oxygen's attractive force causes the uneven distribution of negative charge in all molecules that contain oxygen and hydrogen.

Carbon and hydrogen are comparable in their electronegativities, so there is very little polar character in C-H bonds.

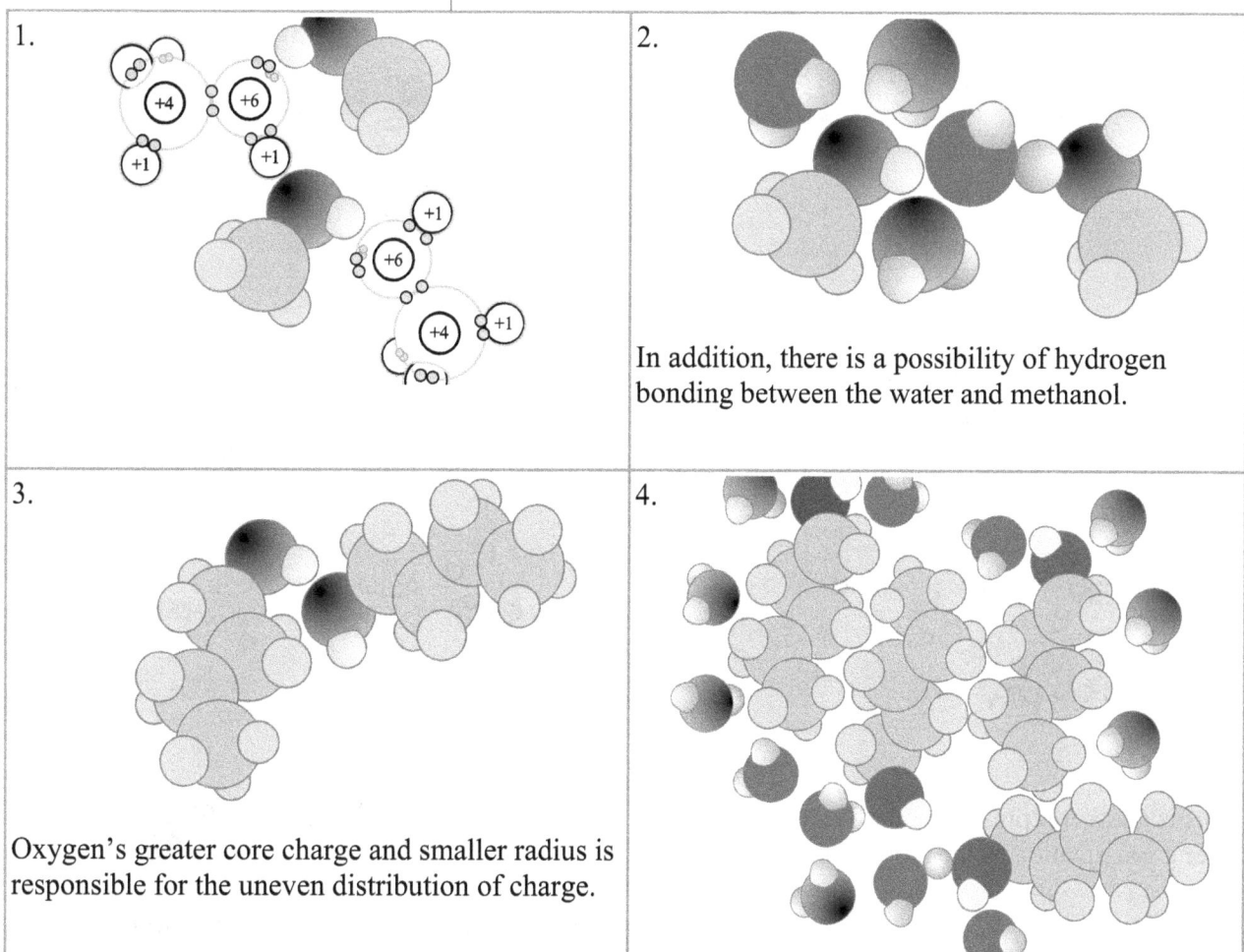

1.

2. In addition, there is a possibility of hydrogen bonding between the water and methanol.

3. Oxygen's greater core charge and smaller radius is responsible for the uneven distribution of charge.

4.

Parents and Teachers
Guide and Resource

Polar Bonds ...

Lab 5.3: Carbonyl Groups as Dipoles

We often require students to combine one schematic structure with another to achieve a more powerful synthesis.

When students combine the "variable speed of the particles" aspect of the particle theory with the "variable force between the particles" aspect, they can explain many more events than either aspect can explain alone.

Pedagogical Issues Most secondary students learn the p-p orbital overlap representation of the π bond in their senior year of high school. Students use this representation to explain the reactivity of double bonds, and the rotational rigidity of alkenes.

Combining that representation with the Ross representation of the atom, we obtain a more dynamic picture of the distribution of electrons within molecules.

Science Issues If oxygen's +6 core charge attracts electrons more strongly than carbon's +4 core charge, then the electron distribution in the π bond will be strongly polarized toward oxygen. Ketones are more polarized than ethers.

1.
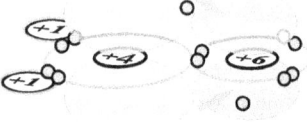
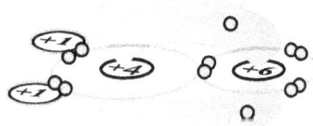

The electrons in the π bonds spend more time near oxygen's +6 core charge.

2.
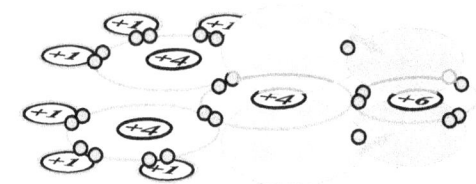

In acetone, the electrons in oxygen's **p** orbital are confined to a smaller average volume by oxygen's +6 core charge.

3.
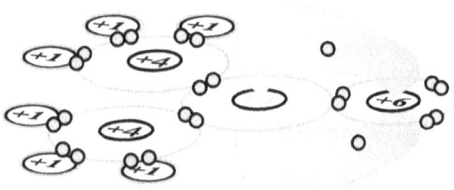

This is another representation of acetone, with the strong polarization of the π bonds emphasized.

4.
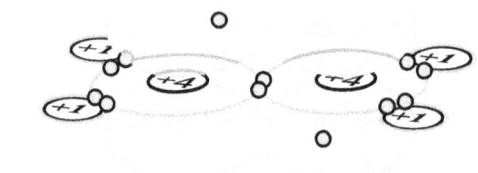
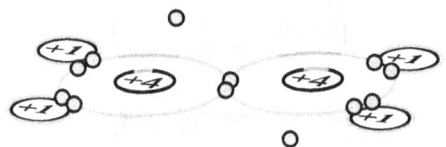

Ethene is non-polar, in contrast with acetone.

... and Dipole Molecules

Ideas About Science and Pedagogy

Quiz 5. Polar Bonds and Dipole Molecules

1. Water molecules are strongly attracted to the ions. Ions thus surrounded by water molecules are separated from each other.

   Any ions that break off from the crystal are quickly "lost in the crowd" of clinging water molecules, and remain dissolved.

   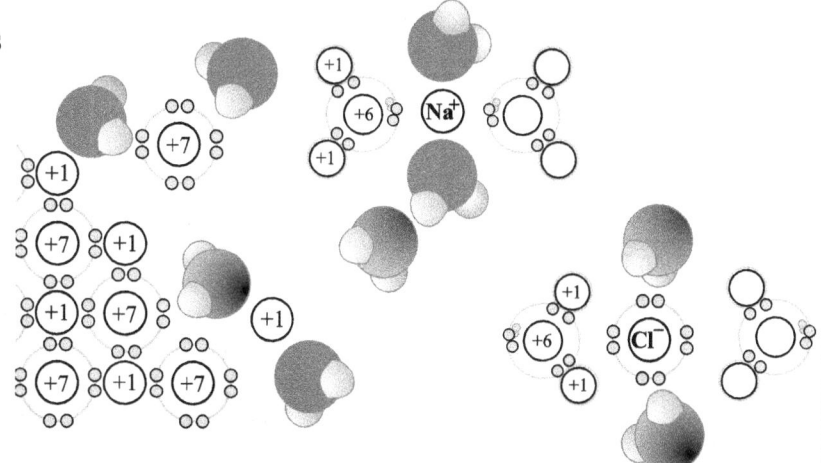

2. Oxygen's large core charge pulls electrons strongly away from hydrogen in both glycerine and in water. The dipoles thus created are attracted to each other

   Glycerine and water dissolve in each other in all proportions

   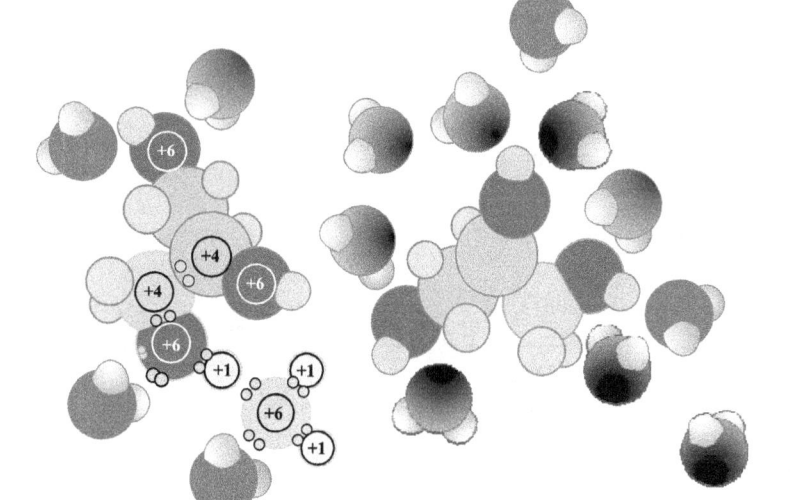

3. Water molecules are always attracted to each other, due to their strongly polar O-H bonds. Hydrogen and carbon have nearly non-polar bonds, and are not strongly attracted to each other. The OH group on butanol will be attracted to water, but the CH bonds will not. Water will tend to stick to itself, and not to the hydrocarbons.

   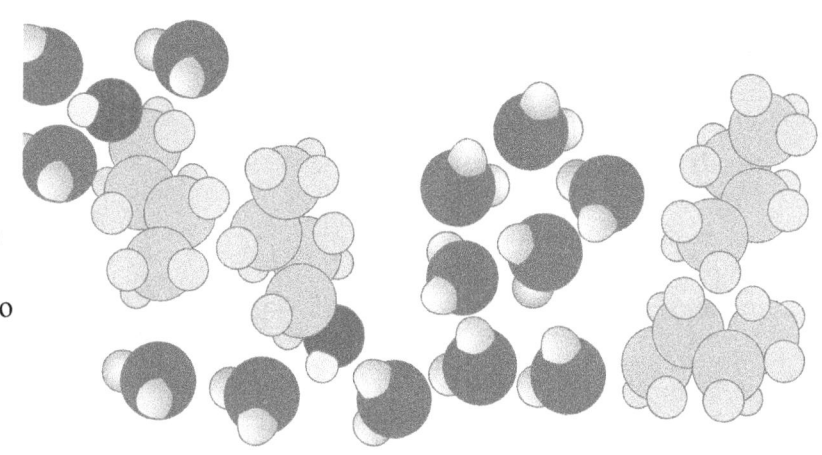

© Ross Lattner Publishing www.rosslattner.ca

Quiz 5: Polar Bonds and Dipole Molecules

4. Iodine is a non-polar molecule. Its covalent electrons are equally attracted to iodine's +7 core charge.

   Water molecules are much more strongly attracted to each other than they are to iodine.

   Result: water sticks strongly to itself, and does not open to let iodine dissolve and diffuse into it.

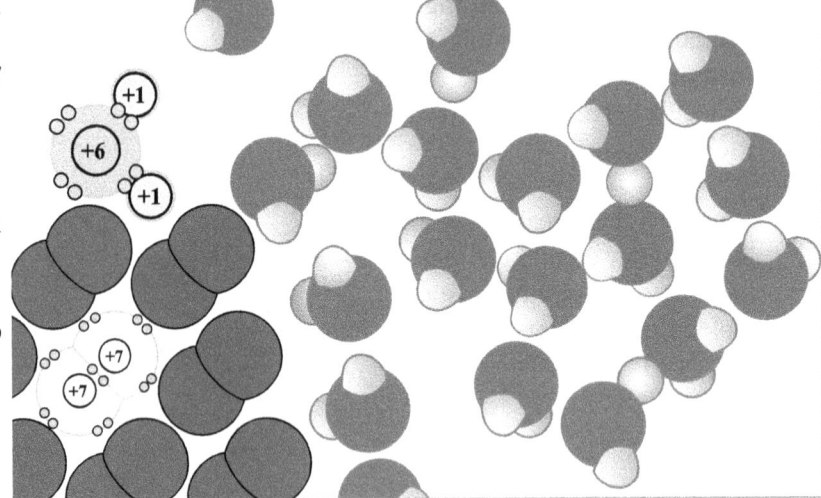

5. The valence electrons in butane are attracted to H and to C almost equally, so butane is not polar. Without dipoles, butane molecules do not stick to each other very strongly. Butane vaporizes in seconds.

   Butanol has just one OH group added to a butane. That polar group attracts others strongly enough that butanol will evaporate more slowly.

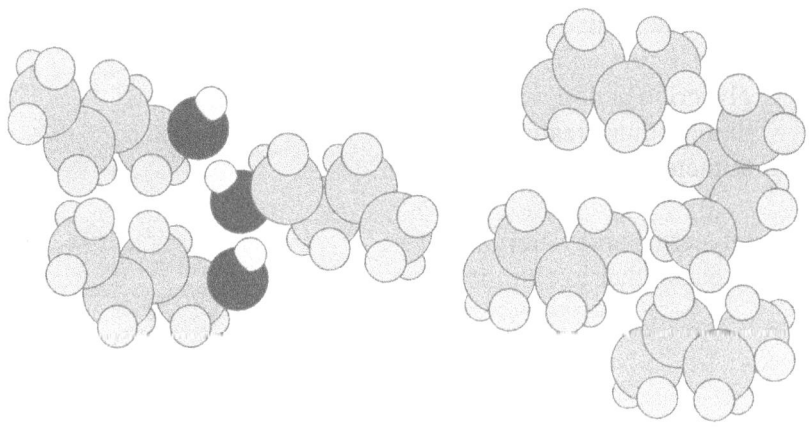

6. The cyclohexane molecules will not be attracted to each other strongly by dipole-dipole interactions. Instead, they will be attracted by the van der Waals forces which act over a large surface area for each molecule. Cyclohexane evaporates easily, and is not attracted to water.

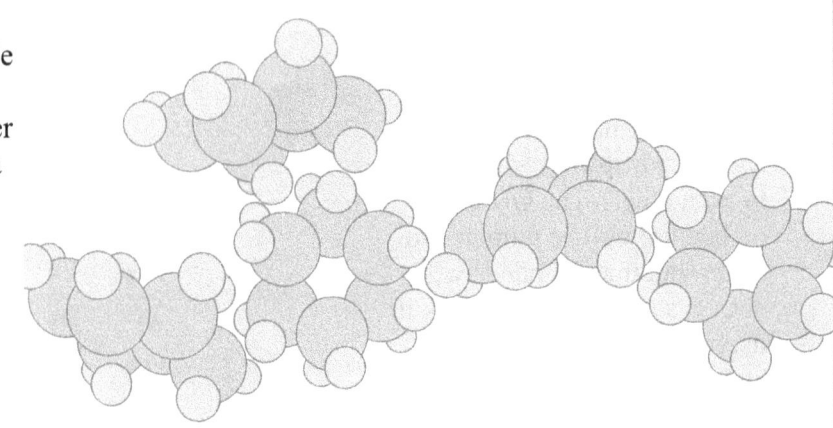

... and Dipole Molecules

Ideas About Science and Pedagogy

Quiz 5: Polar Bonds and Dipole Molecules

7. Both of propanone's the CO bonds are polarized, the σ bond less so than the π bond. Overall, the carbonyl is a very polar region.

   The propanol CO σ bond is equivalent to propanone's, but the OH σ bond is even more polarized. The OH bond makes hydrogen bonding very likely.

   CH_3-CO-CH_3 CH_3-CHOH-CH_3

   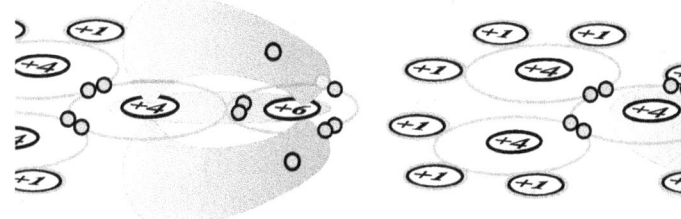

8. Propanone is a ketone. Its carbonyl group is quite polar, but is not as polar as the OH group in 2-propanol. In addition, the OH group in propanol is capable of hydrogen bonding.

   Propanone will vaporize much more readily than propanol.

   CH_3-CO-CH_3 CH_3-CHOH-CH_3

   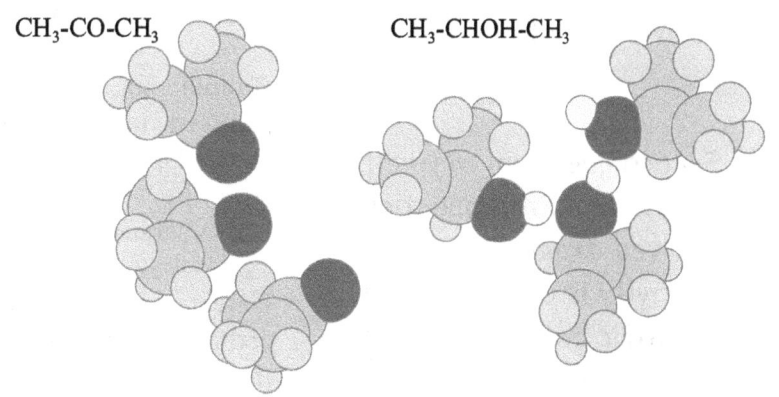

© Ross Lattner Publishing   35   www.rosslattner.ca

The Periodic Table ...

Lab 6.1: Reactions of Non-metal Oxides and Water

"Non-metal oxides dissolve in water to produce acid solutions."

Expressed as a *rule*, this appears to be one of those foundational statements of chemistry. Two questions:

First question: what can a student *do* with this rule? Too frequently, the answer to this question is "she can recite the statement on a test." But that activity is not necessarily science.

Second question: *why* is it true? Answering this question involves *explanation*. This activity is central to the scientific enterprise. The student who is capable of explaining this can answer a great many scientific questions.

Pedagogical Issues

This very familiar lab exercise provides striking evidence that non-metal oxides dissolve in water to produce acidic solutions. The evidence is simple, direct, and dramatic. The best labs consist of simple experiments, requiring mentally challenging explanations.

Science Issues

Safety first. Oxygen accelerates combustion, so use small quantities of carbon and of sulfur. The reactions work reasonably well with air; it's not absolutely necessary to use oxygen.

Be sure to add the indicator before you start the combustion. Consider using other indicators as well:

Bromthymol, plus one tiny crystal of sodium carbonate. The carbonate ion makes the solution basic, and the presence of the acid makes the color change from blue to yellow.

Universal indicator

Universal indicator plus one tiny crystal of sodium carbonate. The colour changes are truly beautiful, especially if you don't swirl the indicator solution.

Here's another option for a demonstration. Generate a *small* amount of NO_2 gas in a volumetric flask. Add a small piece of copper wire to about 5 mL of concentrated nitric acid in a 500 mL volumetric flask. The NO_2 will stay near the bottom of the flask, as it is heavier than air. Pour a tiny amount of the brown gas into a gas bottle prepared as before. The brown gas will dissolve rapidly in water, making a strongly acidic solution.

... and Acid / Base Behaviour

Ideas About Science and Pedagogy

The most weakly bound electrons ● are hydrogen's, with χ = 2.1. Oxygen's electrons ○ are the most strongly bound, with χ = 3.5. The remaining non-metal electrons (sulfur, carbon, bromine, etc.) will be assigned a mid-grey color ◐ because they are in the mid-range.

Lab 6.2: What Makes Non-metal Oxides Acidic?

Pedagogical Issues The structure of the argument here is very similar to the discussion of redox reactions in Activity 2.1 - 2.4 and the related Quiz 2. You may wish to review those activities first.

Science Issues The dividing line between the metals and the non-metals is the metalloids, with a characteristic electronegativity of χ ≈ 2.0. Hydrogen, with χ = 2.1, lies right on the metalloid line: it is more electronegative than the metals, but less electronegative than any other non-metal.

1. Nitric acid

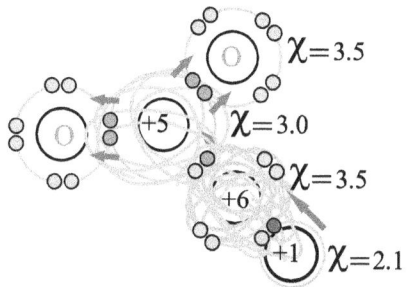

Oxygen is the "big winner," taking electrons from everyone else. Hydrogen is the "big loser." Because it loses its electron, it becomes an H^+ ion

2. Sulfurous acid

Same story. The most loosely held electrons are the most completely removed. In any system of hydrogen, oxygen and any other non-metal, hydrogen must lose its electrons and must become H^+, that is, an acid.

3. Sulfuric acid

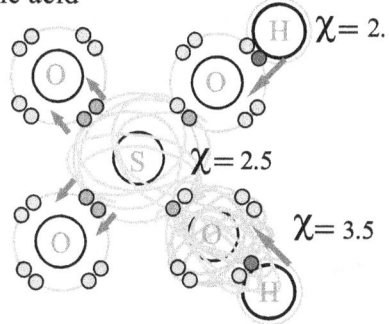

The greatest electron density is found nearest oxygen and sulfur, as they both have core charges of +6 and strongly attract electrons to themselves. Hydrogen is left with the lowest electron density, which makes it acidic.

4. Phosphoric acid

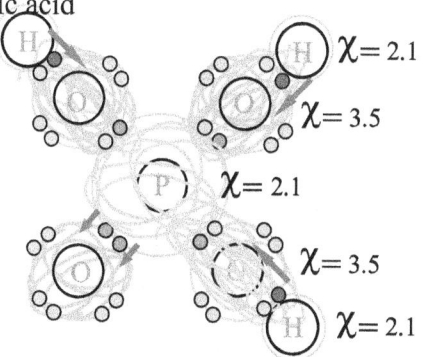

Why does phosphorus, with an electronegativity close to that of hydrogen, make and acid? The four oxygen atoms plus phosphorus in the +5 oxidation state pulls electrons from hydrogen.

© Ross Lattner Publishing www.rosslattner.ca

The Periodic Table ...

Lab 6.3: Reactions of Metal Oxides and Water

Not all metal oxides make basic solutions!

The transition metals are smaller in radius than either Group 1 or Group 2 metals. Transition metals also have a greater core charge than alkali metals or alkali earths.

Consider what happens when a transition metal loses two or three electrons. Small radius. Large core charge. Wants electrons back... Hey, that sounds like a non-metal!

Oxidized transition metals can actually exhibit non-metal behavior! For example, chromium (VI) and manganese (VII) form covalent bonds in dichromate $Cr_2O_7^{2-}$ and permanganate MnO_4^-.

Try this: put a few drops of universal indicator into some water. Add Iron (III) ions... the solution becomes acidic. Also called *hydrolysis*, this phenomenon occurs with small, highly charged metal ions.

Pedagogical Issues

To be effective in a teaching environment, a demonstration or a lab must provide decisive evidence of the phenomenon under study. This pair of demonstrations will do just that, but both of them do take time.

Science Issues

Part A. Safety first. Magnesium burns extremely quickly in oxygen. The reaction is pretty nearly as effective in air.

Be sure to add the indicator before you start the combustion. Consider using other indicators as well:

Bromthymol plus one drop of 0.1 M HCl. The acid makes the indicator yellow, and the metal oxide will change the color from yellow to blue.

Universal indicator plus one drop of 0.1 M HCl. The color changes are beautiful as the solution changes from pink to yellow, green, teal, blue and finally purple.

Part B. Safety First. Two small pieces of calcium metal in a *small* 125 mL Erlenmeyer will react with water to make hydrogen gas. When tested with a flaming wooden splint, the burning hydrogen will produce a loud "whoop."

Both experiments result in the formation of a base. The combination of hydrogen, oxygen and calcium will always eventually settle down into calcium hydroxide, no matter what order you react the elements. Calcium, with a small core charge and large radius, will eventually lose its electrons. Oxygen, with its large core charge and small radius, will eventually gain them. Hydrogen, the "middle ε strength" non-metal element, will always end up covalently bonded to the electronegative oxygen.

Calcium carbonate soils will bring together the elements carbon, oxygen, hydrogen and calcium. Calcium will be the big loser of electrons, and oxygen will be the big winner. Hydrogen is unlikely to lose its electrons to oxygen when large quantities of calcium have given their electrons to oxygen.

... and Acid / Base Behaviour

Ideas About Science and Pedagogy

In a system of metal, oxygen and water, the most weakly bound electrons ● are the metal's, with χ < 2.1. Oxygen's electrons ○ are the most strongly bound, with χ = 3.5.

The remaining non-metal is hydrogen. Its electron will be assigned a mid-grey color ◐ because it is in the mid-range.

Lab 6.4: What Makes Metal Oxides Basic?

Pedagogical Issues Recall the redox reactions involving three elements. The element with the smallest electronegativity χ was always the most oxidized. The element with the greatest χ always ended up reduced. The middle element ended up either isolated, or covalently bonded

Science Issues The dividing line between the metals and the non-metals is the metalloids, with a characteristic electronegativity of χ ≈ 2.0. Hydrogen, with χ = 2.1, lies right on the metalloid line: it is more electronegative than the metals, but less electronegative than any other non-metal.

1. Sodium oxide and water.

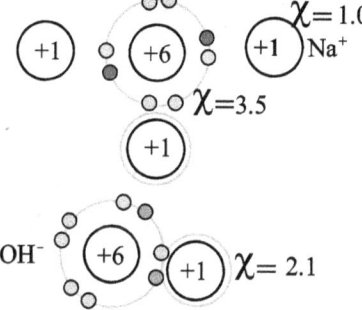

Oxygen strips electrons from Na, creating an O^{2-} ion. The small +1 core charge of hydrogen is now attracted away from the water toward the oxide ion. Note that the OH has 7+ and 8− charges.

2. Calcium and water

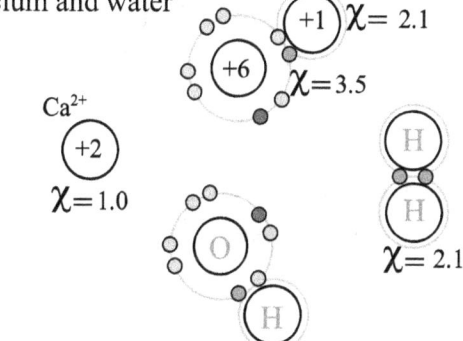

Like taking candy from a baby..Oxygen will take anyone's electrons, but would more readily take them from Ca than from H. Hydrogen pushed off, and two hydroxides created instead. Redox!

3.

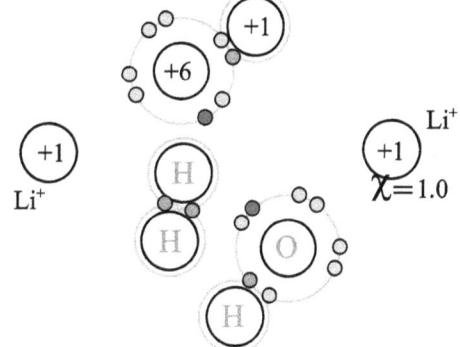

As each oxygen takes the electron offered by the very generous Lithium, oxygen's valence is filled, and hydrogen is pushed off as an element. A redox reaction, this creates two hydroxides.

4.

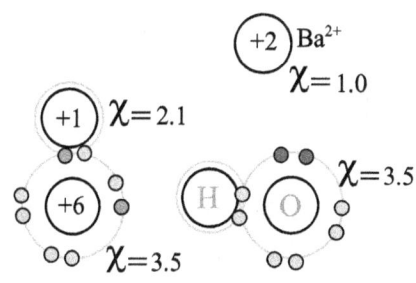

The metal barium has lowest electronegativity. Barium is stripped of its electrons, and those electrons end up in the valence of oxygen. Hydrogen is ends up in a covalent bond.

Parents and Teachers Guide and Resource

The Periodic Table ...

Activity 6.5: Oxidation and Acid Strength

Pedagogical Issues Acid base equilibrium is another of those high hurdles for students. Teachers tend to take one of two approaches to this issue. The first is the formal approach, in which K_a, K_b and K_w are defined, and the acid behavior is described in formal mathematical terms, including equilibrium equations. The second is a conceptual approach, in which the acid / base equilibrium is described as a competition for protons within a system of more or less "hungry" bases.

The Ross description of chemical bonding provides support for the second approach.

Science Issues

The acid constant, K_a, is, precisely speaking, an equilibrium constant for the reaction in which water takes a proton from an acid. In science classes, the acid constant is usually understood as a measure of the tendency of an acid to donate a proton to water.

In this exercise, we are trying to relate the K_a to the properties of the atoms of which the acids are composed. Two factors are emphasized: the electronegativity of the central atom, and the oxidation state of the central atom.

The oxidation state itself depends upon the number of oxygen atoms present. The small radius of each oxygen atom causes electrons to move toward the oxygen. Ultimately, electrons are drawn away from the hydrogens.

This exercise presents a challenge to students. How can we account for K_a values?

It is clear that the Ross model of the atom can account for some of the variation in K_a.

However, the correlation is only partial. Other factors must be involved. Size of the overall ion? Charge distribution over the dissociated ion?

Get students involved in the speculation!

Increasing the oxidation number of the sulfur by +2 appears to cause the K_a to increase by a factor of 10^8

Note that the lone pair on the sulfurous acid can be drawn into the sulfur, reducing the electrostatic attraction upon the OH bonding electrons.

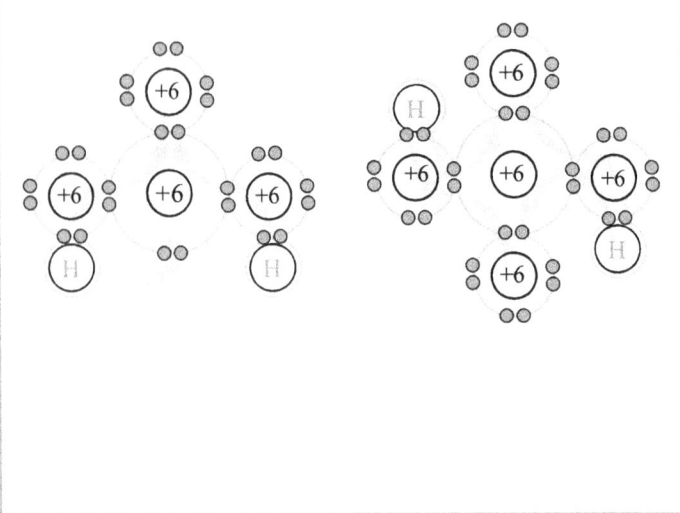

Acid	χ_x	$\varnothing_x$	K_a
Sulfurous H_2SO_3	2.5	+4	2×10^{-2}
Sulfuric H_2SO_4	2.5	+6	$2 \times 10^{+6}$

... and Acid / Base Behaviour

Ideas About Science and Pedagogy

Similar to the sulfuric / sulfurous pair, increasing the oxidation number by +2 increases K_a by about 10^6.

Still, there is difference. The increase this time is smaller by a factor of 100. Why?

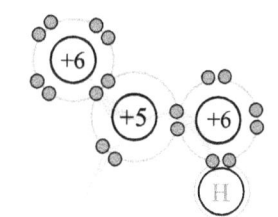

Acid	χ_x	$\varnothing_x$	K_a
Nitric HNO_3	3.0	+5	200
Nitrous HNO_2	3.0	+3	2×10^{-4}

This pair is a trend breaker.
Both χ_x and $\varnothing_x$ are the same.
So why are these K_a's so different?

Neither of these acids can be isolated. They are only present in equilibrium with solutions of the gases CO_2 and SO_2. Perhaps the % of gas that combines with water and dissociates is different....

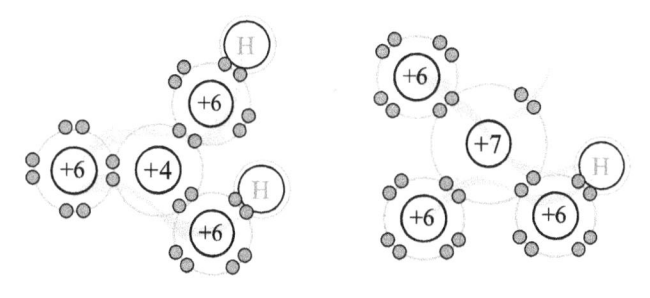

Acid	χ_x	$\varnothing_x$	K_a
Carbonic H_2CO_3	2.5	+4	4×10^{-7}
Sulfurous H_2SO_3	2.5	+4	2×10^{-2}

The nitrogen and chlorine are similar in electronegativity and in oxidation number.

They differ in two ways: the chlorine has one additional non-bonded pair. As this additional pair is attracted into the chlorine, it appears to reduce the K_a by a factor of about 20.

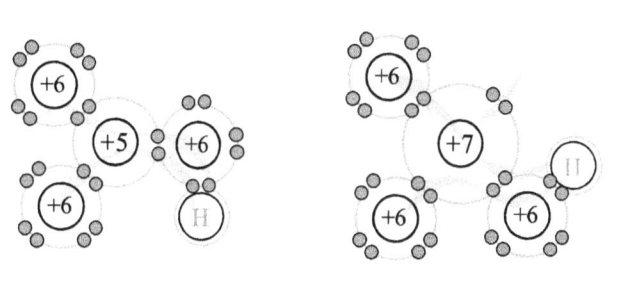

Acid	χ_x	$\varnothing_x$	K_a
Nitric HNO_3	3.0	+5	200
Chloric $HClO_3$	3.0	+5	10

Table Talk

Student Exercises and Labs

Knowledge and Understanding

You will learn to use pictures to represent things that you cannot see. Your pictures, even though they may not be scientifically complete, can help you think clearly about the things you can see in your experiments. In particular, you will learn how do draw diagrams of atoms including their atomic cores, valence electrons, and radius..

Knowledge and understanding are probed at regular intervals in the *How Good Is Your Table Talk?* quizzes. Study these as you go through the exercises, so that you can do your best when they are assigned.

Inquiry and Thinking

We will use the PEOE (Predict Explain Observe Explain) cycle for most labs and activities. You are expected to frame a question, provide your best prediction, and explain your thinking, using both sentences and diagrams.

At the end of the unit, you should be able to use the Ross representation of the atom to help you construct good questions and hypotheses about many everyday events.

Communication

The quality of your arguments is the most important aspect of communication in this chapter. Your arguments consist of sentences, organized into paragraphs, and supported by diagrams or other representations.

Each sentence should be clear and to the point. You will find it best to limit your sentences to two concepts linked together to make a reasonable claim. If you need to relate more than two concepts, add a new sentence.

Applications, Connections and Extensions

Every exercise in this book is designed to support you as you learn appropriate theories and apply them to problems. In the labs, you demonstrate your understanding of a theory only by applying the theory. In the quizzes and projects, you are invited to make further connections and extensions of your learning.

Table Talk — Student Exercises
Who Gets the Electron ...

Activity 1.1: Gaining Electrons is Reduction

What's The Question? Non-metals are the most electronegative elements (greatest core charges and smallest radii) They are able to take electrons from other atoms. In the process, the non-metals become negatively charged. Chemists say that elements which *gain electrons* are *reduced*.

When they are reduced, what oxidation states ⦵ do the non-metals achieve?

What Are We Doing?	What Are We Thinking About?
1. Consider an atom of bromine, near a source of electrons. 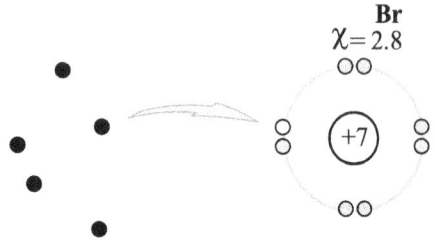 2. The electrons are strongly attracted into the valence shell by the large core charge and the small radius. Because there is only one vacancy in the valence shell, the atom will attract and hold one electron. 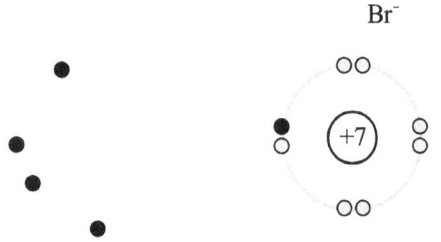 The *bromine atom* has become a *bromide ion*. It has been "reduced" to the −1 oxidation state. It will not attract and hold any more electrons, so it cannot be reduced further.	• In ionic compounds, *oxidation state* ⦵ is the *charge on an ion*, indicating the number of electrons lost or gained. • in covalent molecules, oxidation number ⦵ is the formal number of electrons "lost" (moved away from) or "gained" (moved toward) an atom as it formed bonds with other atoms. • When an element is "reduced", it gains electrons, and its oxidation number ⦵ is decreased. 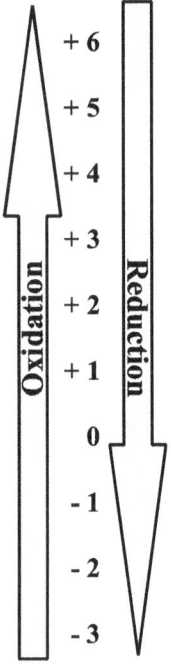 **Oxidation Number** Formal number of electrons "lost" or "gained" in bonds to other atoms

- The total charge on the bromine atom can be calculated by adding the core charge, plus the electrons in the valence shell. For the bromine *atom*, Br, (top left picture) the ⦵ is zero.

  Br⦵ = (core) + (valence)
  = (+7) + (−7)
  = 0

- the ⦵ of the bromide *ion* is found in the same way. Add up the core charge (+7) and the valence electrons (−8).

  Br⦵ = (core) + (valence)
  = (+7) + (−8)
  = −1

- Non-metals tend to gain electrons until their valence shells are filled.

... Oxidation States

Name:
Date:

Complete each row of the table below to show the element name, valence electrons, core charge, oxidation state and ion name.

	Diagram of non-metal gaining electrons	Final oxidation state	Name
1 	Fluorine (+7)	∅ = (core) + (valence) = ( ) + ( ) =	Fluoride F⁻
2	Sulfur (+6)	∅ = (core) + (valence) = ( ) + ( ) =	
3 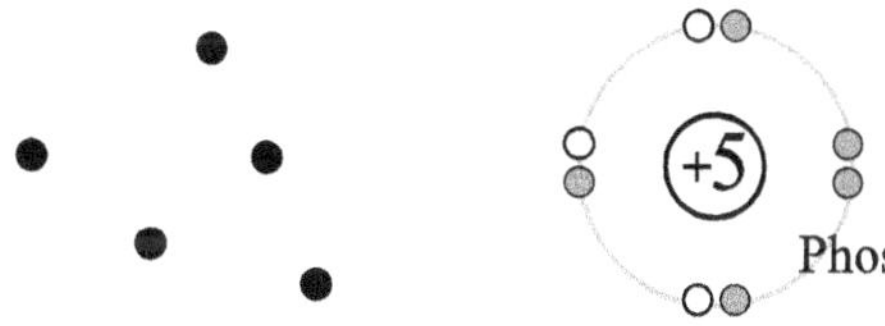	Phosphorus (+5)		
4			Oxide O²⁻
5			N³⁻

© Ross Lattner Publishing www.rosslattner.ca

Table Talk
Student Exercises

Who Loses Electrons ...

Activity 1.2: Losing Electrons is Oxidation

What's The Question? Metals are characterized by small core charges, and large radii. They only have a few electrons, and they don't hold onto them very tightly. Metals are easily oxidized, that is, they can lose electrons easily.

What oxidation states Ø do the Group 1, Group 2 and Group 13 elements achieve?

What Are We Doing?	*What Are We Thinking About?*
1. Consider an atom of sodium, near a number of fluorine atoms. 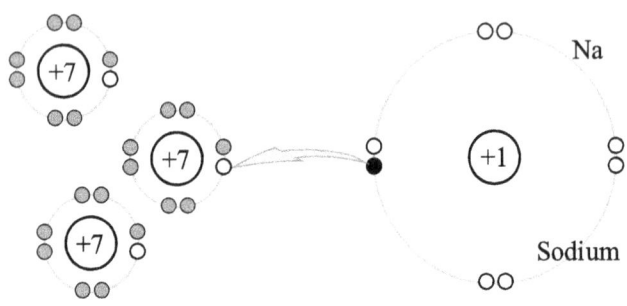 2. Sodium's only electron is weakly attracted to the sodium +1 core, but it is strongly attracted to fluorine. Sodium will lose its only electron. 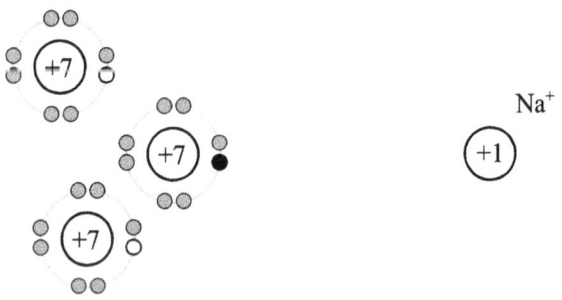 The sodium atom has been oxidized to Ø = +1. It is now a sodium *ion*. It has no more valence electrons, so it cannot be oxidized further.	• Which arrow represents *oxidation*? Which arrow represent *reduction*? Label the arrows. • Oxidation is loss of electrons. • Reduction is gain of electrons. • Print the symbol for each ion formed in activities 1.1 and 1.2 on the matching oxidation number in the diagram above.

+6
+5
+4
+3
+2
+1
0
-1
-2
-3

- The total charge on the sodium *atom* is calculated by adding the core charge, plus the electrons in the valence shell. For the sodium atom, Na, (top left picture) the Ø = zero.

  NaØ = (core) + (valence)
       = (+1)+(−1)
       = 0

- the oxidation state of the sodium *ion* is found in the same way. Add up the core charge (+1) and the valence electrons (−0).

  NaØ = (core) + (valence)
       = (+1)+(−0)
       = +1

© Ross Lattner Publishing   www.rosslattner.ca

...Oxidation States

Name:
Date:

Diagram of metal losing electrons	Final oxidation state	Name
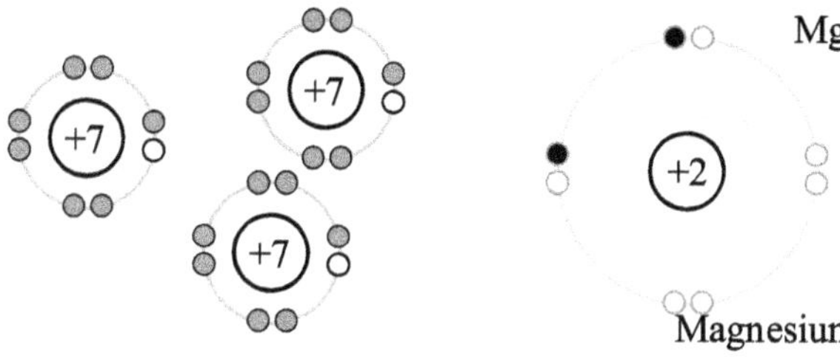 Mg Magnesium	∅ = (core) + (valence) = ( ) + ( ) =	Magnesium ion Mg^{+2}
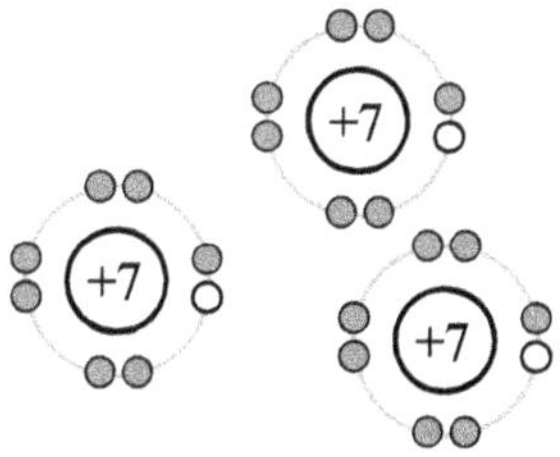 Al Aluminum	∅ = (core) + (valence) = ( ) + ( ) =	
		Lithium ion
		Ca^{2+}
		Gallium ion

© Ross Lattner Publishing 47 www.rosslattner.ca

Table Talk
Student Exercises

Determining Formal ...

Activity 1.3: Determining Formal Oxidation Numbers

What's The Question? How do we figure out the oxidation number of an element within a compound?

What Are We Thinking About? First thing to do... memorize these seven rules.

1. Pure elements have oxidation state $\varnothing = 0$.

Aluminum: Core charge +3, valence −3.

Fluorine: in the tug of war for electrons, it's a tie. Neither fluorine atom wins or loses an electron.

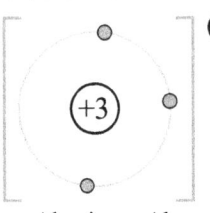
Aluminum, Al

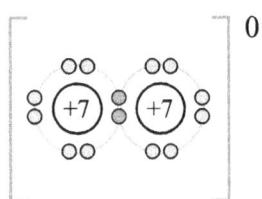
Fluorine, F_2

2. Ions: Oxidation state is same as charge.

Ca^{2+} has ionic charge = $\varnothing$ = +2.

Cl^- has ionic charge = $\varnothing$ = −1

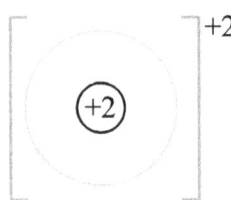
Calcium, Ca^{2+}

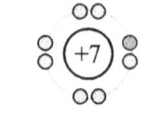
Chloride, Cl^-

3. Metals lose their valence electrons
　　Group 1 ions have $\varnothing$ = +1
　　Group 2 ions have $\varnothing$ = +2
　　Group 13 ions have $\varnothing$ = +3
These metals lose all of their valence electrons to form positive ions. In fact, there is nothing left but the cores

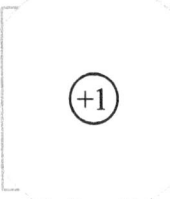
Sodium, Na^+

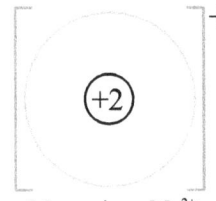
Magnesium, Mg^{2+}

Aluminum, Al^{3+}

4. Non metals fill their valence shells
　　Group 17 ions have $\varnothing$ = −1
　　Group 16 ions have $\varnothing$ = −2
　　Group 15 ions have $\varnothing$ = −3
Non-metals gain electrons until their valence shells are filled. They can *also* lose valence electrons and get $\varnothing$ = +.

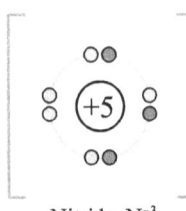
Nitride, N^{-3}

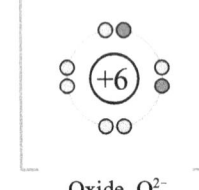
Oxide, O^{2-}

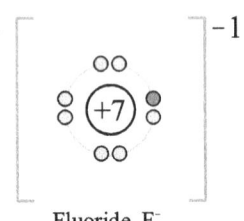
Fluoride, F^-

5. Oxygen $\varnothing$ = −2. e.g. H_2O. In the tug of war for electrons, oxygen wins two electrons... one from each of the hydrogens.

Except peroxides, $\varnothing$ = −1. e.g. H_2O_2. In the tug of war for electrons, each oxygen wins one from hydrogen. The two oxygens tie with each other.

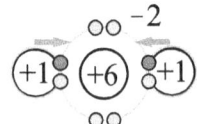
Water, H_2O

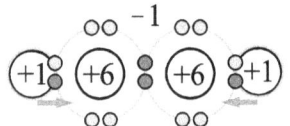
Hydrogen Peroxide H_2O_2

... Oxidation States

Name:
Date:

6. Hydrogen ∅ = +1. In any compound with a non-metal, hydrogen invariably loses the tug of war for electrons. Hydrogen is usually in a +1 state.

Except metal hydrides, ∅ = −1. Metals have a weak hold on their electrons. In the tug of war for electrons, hydrogen wins, metals lose.

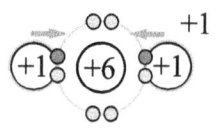
Water, H_2O

Magnesium Hydride, MgH_2

7. Total of all oxidation states = total charge on molecule.

With these rules, you can find the oxidation number of any element in most compounds. What is the oxidation state of chromium in potassium chromate, K_2CrO_4? Set the problem up like a book-keeping situation. To find the oxidation number of chromium, you must set up a total. You know K, O and the total. Find Cr.

$2\ K\ @\ +1 = +2$
$1\ Cr\ @\ +6 = +6$
$4\ O\ @\ -2 = -8$
Total $= 0$

If the molecule has a charge, like the sulfate ion, SO_4^{2-}, the problem is essentially the same. You know O, and you know the total.

What number must sulfur be so that the total equals −2 ?

$1\ S\ @\ +6 = +6$
$4\ O\ @\ -2 = -8$
Total $= -2$

What Are We Doing? Write the oxidation number below each element in the following compounds.

1. H_2S +1 −2	5. P_4O_{10}	9. $KMnO_4$	13. PO_4^{3-}
2. SO_2	6. H_2SO_4	10. HCN	14. NO_2^-
3. NH_3	7. K_2SO_3	11. ClO_3^-	15. CO_3^{2-}
4. NO_2	8. $NaNO_3$	12. SO_3^{2-}	16. IO_4^-

Table Talk
Student Exercises

When you lose more than one ...

Activity 1.4: Elements With More Than One Oxidation State

What's The Question? Some elements have more than one positive oxidation state. Iodine, for example, can gain one electron (be reduced) to the −1 oxidation state. Iodine can also lose electrons (be oxidized) to the +1, +3, +5, and even the +7 state.
How is it possible to have more than one positive oxidation state?

What Are We Thinking About?

Let's start with separate fluorine and iodine atoms. The unpaired valence electron in iodine is close to a +7 core charge (dark colour). The unpaired electron in fluorine is even closer to a +7 core charge. Both unpaired electrons could be shared by the atoms, making them close to *two* core charges.	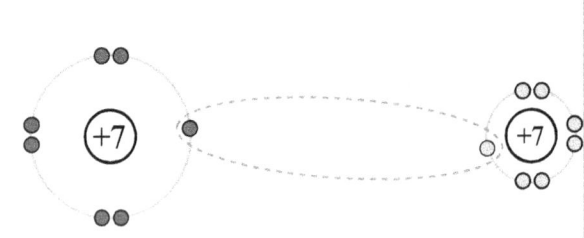
In the tug of war between I and F, iodine is weaker, and fluorine is stronger. Iodine's electron is pulled toward fluorine. Iodine "loses" the electron and is oxidized to the +1 state. Fluorine "gains" the electron and is reduced to ∅ = −1.	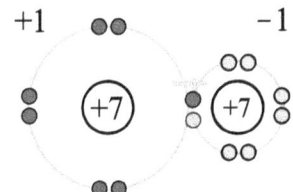
If there is enough fluorine present, the fluorines can split up another pair of iodine's electrons, and share those. Now iodine has lost three electrons. Each fluorine has gained one. Iodine ∅ = +3 Fluorine ∅ = −1 .	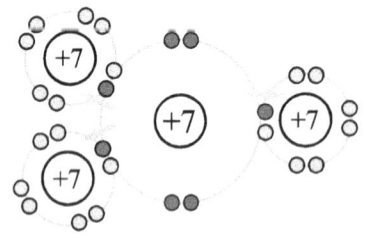
Iodine oxidized to an even higher state: +5! To form the covalent bond, two fluorines must split another non-bonding pair of valence electrons on the iodine atom, then attract them into their smaller radius. Can iodine be oxidized further? Explain!	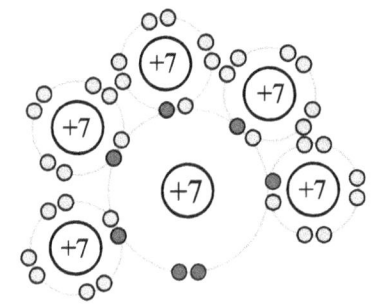

... Multiple Oxidation States

Name:
Date:

1. Nitrogen can form NF_3 and NF_5. Draw Ross diagrams to show the molecules, and print the oxidation state of nitrogen on each one.

2. Phosphorus is known to form compounds with $\varnothing = +3$ and $\varnothing = +5$. How is this possible? Use P and F as your examples.

3. Water is H_2O. Hydrogen peroxide is H_2O_2. What are the oxidation states of oxygen in those two molecules? Draw Ross diagrams to illustrate your answer.

4. In tellurium (II) chloride, $TeCl_2$, tellurium has $\varnothing = +2$. Draw the molecule and explain the oxidation state.

5. In tellurium (IV) chloride, $TeCl_4$, tellurium $\varnothing = +4$. Draw the molecule. Explain.

6. Sulfur can form SF_2, SF_4 and SF_6. Draw all three. Write the oxidation states of sulfur.

Table Talk
Student Exercises

Polyatomic Ions ...

Activity 1.5: Oxidation Numbers in Common Polyatomic Ions

What's The Question? Polyatomic ions are groups of atoms that have an overall ionic charge. Some common examples are carbonate ion, CO_3^{2-} and sulfate ion, SO_4^{2-}.

What are the oxidation states ∅ of the elements in such ions?

What Are We Thinking About?
- Use the Lewis Dot system for determining the electron structure of a covalent molecule.
- Check all your answers using the seven rules for formal oxidation states.

What Are We Doing? Find all oxidation numbers.
Example 1: Carbonate ion CO_3^{2-}

Twenty four electrons are found in the carbonate ion. Four were contributed by carbon (medium grey ◕). Eighteen were provided by the three oxygens (light grey ○). Two extra electrons make up the 2- overall charge on the ion (dark grey ●).

Win, lose or tie in the tug of war for electrons?

- Carbon is the big loser. Its four valence electrons are all pulled toward O atoms. ∅ = +4

- Each oxygen keeps all of its own electrons, and wins two more. ∅ = -2

Example 2: Chlorate ion ClO_3^-

Count electrons. Chlorine provided seven ◕, each oxygen provided six ○, and one additional electron accounts for the overall charge ●.
Note: chlorine has a slightly greater core charge, but oxygen has a much smaller radius. Electrons tend toward oxygen.

Win lose or tie? Chlorine "loses" five of its electrons to the surrounding oxygens. Chlorine ∅ = +5.

Each oxygen wins two electrons. Oxygen ∅ = -2.

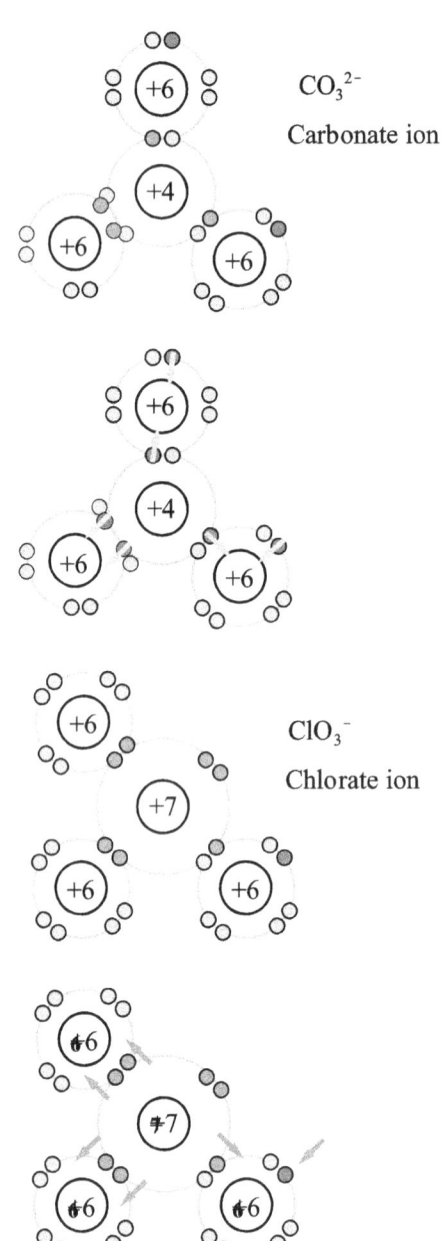

CO_3^{2-}
Carbonate ion

ClO_3^-
Chlorate ion

© Ross Lattner Publishing   www.rosslattner.ca

... and Their Oxidation States

Name:
Date:

1. Hypoiodite ion is simple... IO^-.

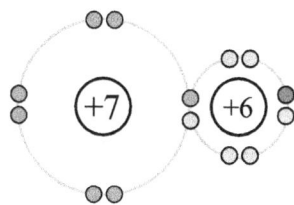

Draw arrows to show which electrons are displaced. What is the ⊘ for each atom?

2. Iodite has one more oxygen. IO_2^-

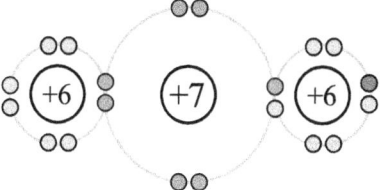

Find the oxidation state ⊘ for each atom.

3. What is the ⊘ of each atom in Iodate?

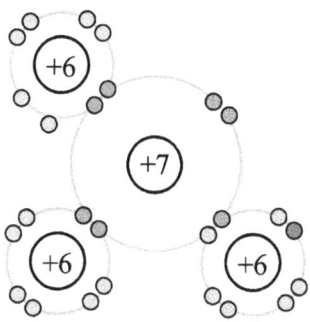

4. Find ⊘ for the atoms in Periodate IO_4^-.

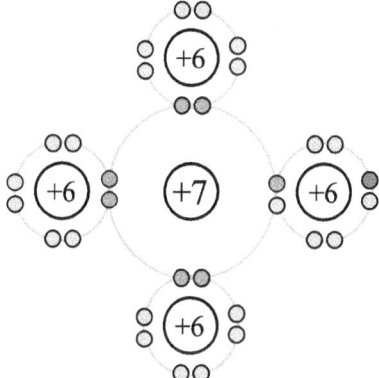

5. Phosphate PO_4^{3-} is essential for life. What is ⊘ of each element?

6. Sulfite is SO_3^{2-} forms when sulfur dioxide dissolves in rain. Find all ⊘.

You can say something nice, dear, if you think long enough

How Good is your Table Talk?

Quiz 1: Oxidation States

1. Al and Cl form white, crystalline AlCl₃. Complete the Ross diagram. Draw arrows to show electron transfer. 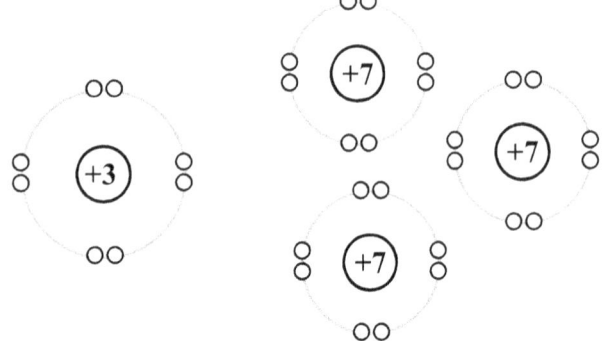	2. H and S combine to form H₂S, a toxic gas that smells of rotten eggs and swamps. Complete the Ross diagrams. Draw a diagram to show the molecule. 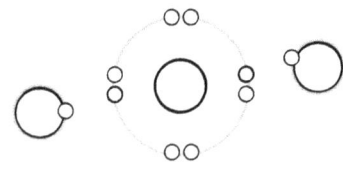
Date: _____ / 5	Date: _____ / 5

3. Calculate ∅ for each element in AlCl₃. Show your work. Complete the table to summarize.
 	
                          χ   ∅
 Aluminum   ☐   ☐
 Chlorine   ☐   ☐
	4. Calculate ∅ for each element in H₂S. Show your work. Complete the table to summarize.
	
	                          χ ∅
	 Hydrogen ☐ ☐
	 Sulfur ☐ ☐

Date: _____ / 5	Date: _____ / 5

You can say something nice, dear, if you think long enough

How Good is your Table Talk?

Quiz 1: Oxidation States Name:

---

5 Shown below is a sulfur atom, and a source of free electrons.

a) Show movement of electrons with arrows.
b) Draw and name the resultant ion.
c) Find ∅ for the resultant ion.

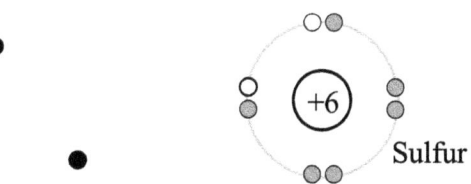

Sulfur

Date: _____ / 5

---

6 Sulfur dioxide is held together with covalent bonds as shown below.

a) Label the atoms. Whose electrons are pulled away? Why?

b) Show movement of electrons with arrows.

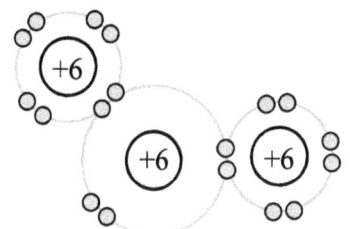

c) Write ∅ for each atom.

Date: _____ / 5

---

7 The sulfite ion SO_3^{2-} is shown below.

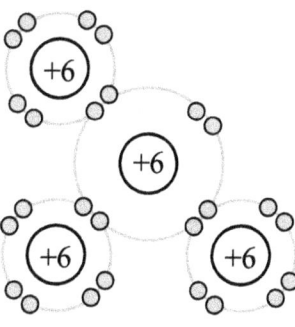

Calculate ∅ for each element. Write ∅ next to each atom. Show all of your work below.

Date: _____ / 5

---

8 Draw a Ross diagram of the sulfate ion SO_4^{2-} below.

Calculate ∅ for each element. Write ∅ next to each atom. Show all of your work below.

Date: _____ / 5

You can say something nice, dear, if you think long enough

How Good is your Table Talk?

Quiz 1: Oxidation States   **Name:**

9 Calculate ⌀ for each element in the compound xenon tetrafluoride, XeF_4. Show all of your work.

Date: _____   / 5

10 Phosphorus trifluoride PF_3 is a colorless liquid used in the manufacture of pesticides. Find ⌀ for each element in the compound. Show all of your work.

Date: _____   / 5

11 Phosphorus pentachloride PCl_5 is a slightly yellow solid, and is known to be toxic. What is ⌀ for each element in the compound? Show your work.

Date: _____   / 5

12 Phosphate ion, PO_4^{3-} is used in all of the processes that underlie life. Find ⌀ for each element in the compound. Show your work.

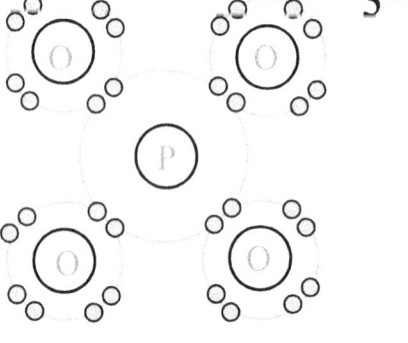

Date: _____   / 5

You can say something nice, dear, if you think long enough

How Good is your Table Talk?

Quiz 1: Oxidation States Name:

---

13 Hydrogen cyanide, HCN, is an extremely toxic gas. Find $\varnothing$ for each element in the compound. Show your work.

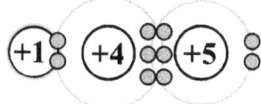

Date: / 5

---

14 Label each atom N, C, H or O. Find $\varnothing$ for each element in the compound hydrogen cyanate. Show your work.

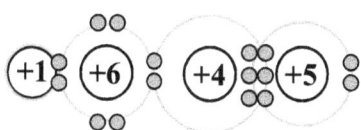

Date: / 5

---

15 Common chlorine bleach contains hypochlorous acid, HOCl. What is the oxidation state of each element?

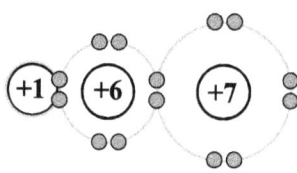

Date: / 5

---

16 Label each atom N, C, H or S in hydrogen thiocyanate. Find $\varnothing$ for each element. Show your work.

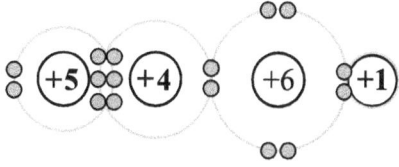

Date: / 5

© Ross Lattner Publishing   57   www.rosslattner.ca

Table Talk
Student Exercises
Winning and losing ...

Activity 2.1: The Essential Concepts of Redox Reactions

Do you Remember? Complete the core - valence - radius diagrams below.

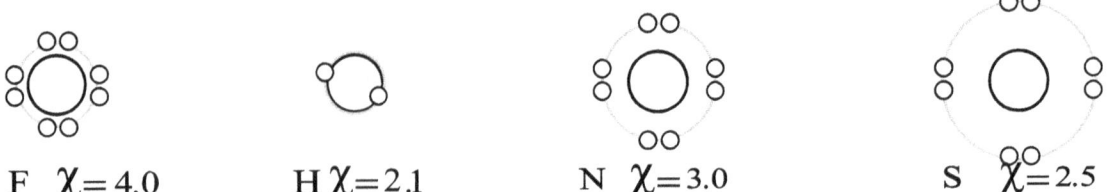

F χ = 4.0   H χ = 2.1   N χ = 3.0   S χ = 2.5

What's The Question? Redox reactions are chemical changes in which **red**uction and **ox**idation occur. Electrons must move away from one element (oxidation) and toward another (reduction). *How do we represent a redox reaction? What new concepts are necessary?*

What Are We Thinking About?
- In all redox reactions, the ∅ of one species increases, and the ∅ of another species decreases.
- We will use arrows to represent the change of oxidation numbers ∅.

What Are We Doing? Study each reaction in the examples below:
1. Find the oxidation number of each element below in every occurrence (see grey band).
2. Identify the elements that have changed oxidation numbers.
3. Trace the arrows to indicate the changes in oxidation number.
4. Check the total number of electrons "lost" and "gained" in the overall reaction.
5. Identify the *oxidizing agent* and the *reducing agent*.

```
         reducing agent        oxidizing agent

            1 H₂                  1 F₂         ⇒        2 HF
   ∅ =       0                     0                    +1  -1
                                        gain 2 electrons. Reduced
                         lose 2 electrons. Oxidized
```

Here's another example:

```
         oxidizing agent       reducing agent

            3 F₂        +        1 N₂         ⇒        2 NF₃
   ∅ =       0                     0                   +3  -1
                                        lose 6 electrons. oxidized
                         gain 6 electrons. reduced
```

... Redox Reactions

Name:
Date:

Practice Exercises Complete these chemical equations to show all of the following:
- Write the oxidation number of each element in every occurrence.
- Balance each chemical equation.
- Draw oxidation and reduction arrows, and indicate how many electrons were "lost" and "gained"
- Label the *oxidizing agent* and the *reducing agent*.

1

_____ agent   _____ agent

____ H_2 +   ____ N_2 ⇒   ____ NH_3

∅ =

2

_____ agent   _____ agent

____ S   +   ____ F_2 ⇒   ____ SF_4

∅ =

3

____ S   +   ____ F_2 ⇒   ____ SF_6

4

____ N_2 +   ____ F_2 ⇒   ____ NF_5

Questions For Later...

1. Compare the core charge and radius of the oxidizing agent to the reducing agent in each case. What patterns can you discern? Explain your thinking.

2. The oxidizing agent is always reduced. The reducing agent is always oxidized. Why is this?

Table Talk
Student Exercises

Who Gets the Electron ...

Activity 2.2: Redox Reactions Between Metals and Non-Metals

What's The Question? How do scientists represent redox reactions between metals and non-metals?

What Are We Thinking About?
- Study the reaction between lithium metal and fluorine gas.
- Fluorine starts off as a diatomic molecule. Each fluorine shares one of the other's electrons.
- If the fluorine covalent bond is broken, each fluorine can grab one electron from one lithium.
- Each fluorine gains 1 e⁻, becoming a F⁻ ion. Each lithium loses 1 e⁻, becoming a Li⁺ ion.
- These F⁻ ions and Li⁺ ions, together with many others, make a crystal lattice.

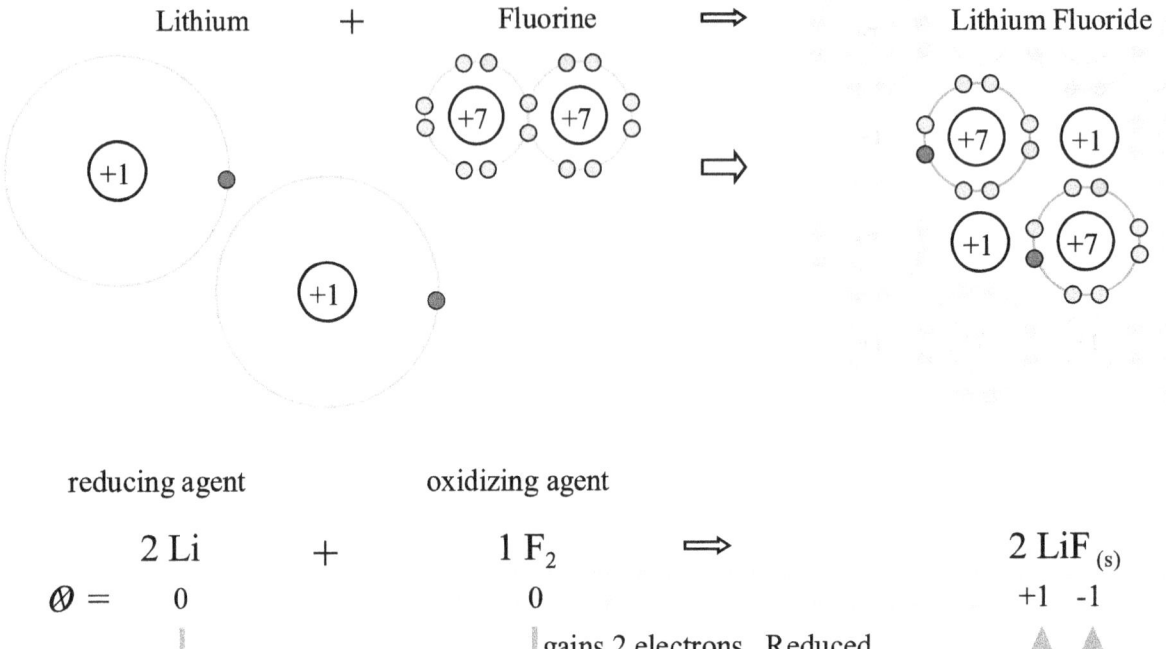

- Note: The valence electron in lithium was very far from the core. Once Li lost that electron, only the tiny core remained, about the size of the helium atom. The fluoride and lithium ions then make up the crystal lattice. Only two units of the crystal lattice are emphasized in the diagram above.

Questions For Later...
1. Redox reactions between metals and non-metals frequently result in ionic crystal lattices like those in the examples. Explain why, using the core valence radius model.

2. If aluminum lost its three valence electrons, what would be left? About how big would it be? Explain.

... Redox Reactions

Name:
Date:

What Are We Doing? In the two exercises below, add words, numbers and diagrams as needed to complete the diagrams like the examples on the previous page.

1

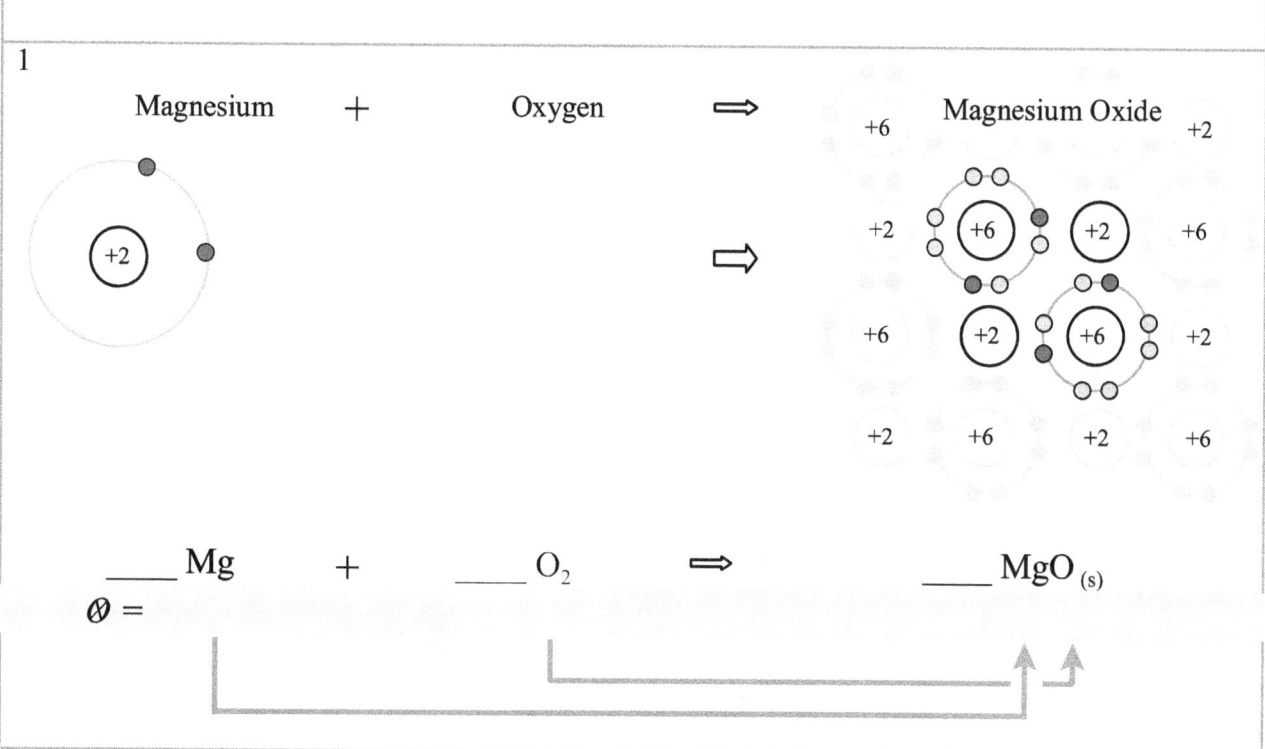

____ Mg   +   ____ O_2 ⇒   ____ MgO$_{(s)}$

⊘ =

2

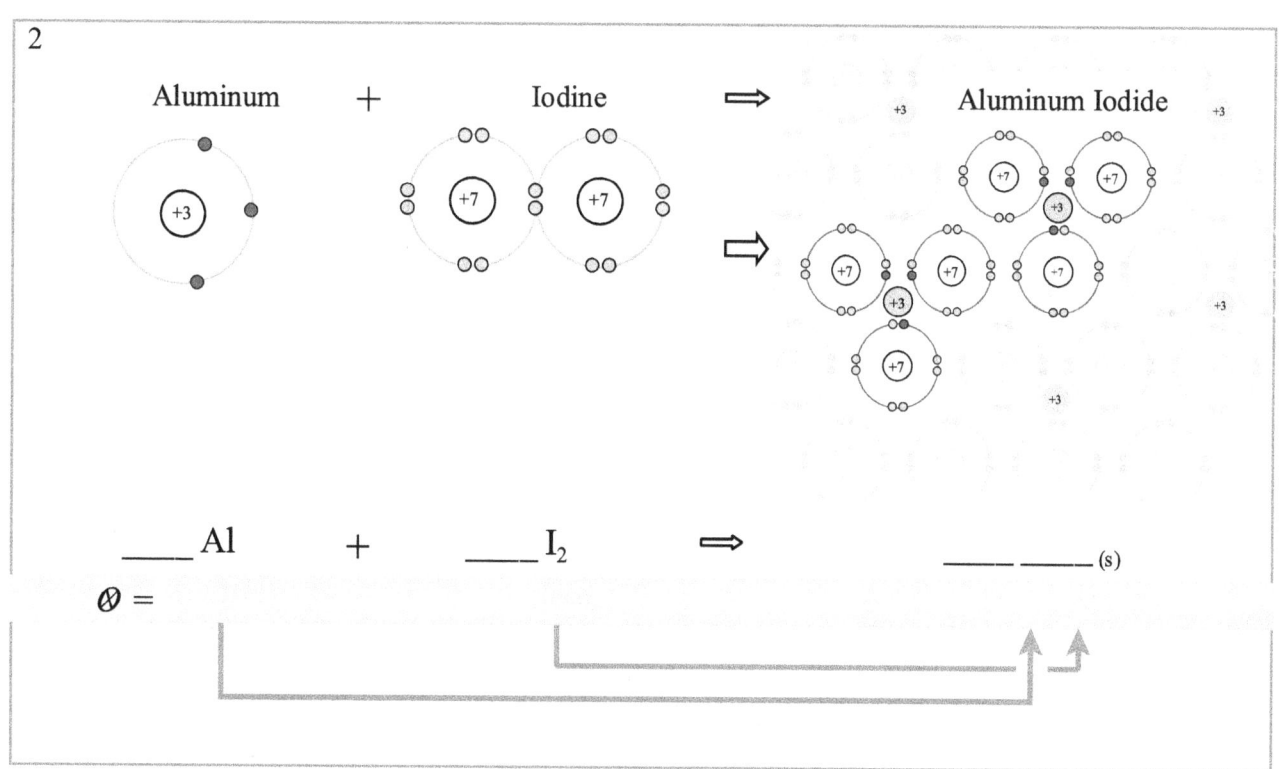

____ Al   +   ____ I_2 ⇒   ____ ____$_{(s)}$

⊘ =

Table Talk
Student Exercises

Who Loses Electrons ...

Activity 2.3: Redox Reactions Among Non-metal Elements

What's The Question? Non-metals form covalent compounds. The electron pairs in covalent bonds are often shared unequally, so that one of the elements "loses" an electron to the other.
How do the electrons move during a redox reaction among non-metals?

What Are We Thinking About?
- Study the bonding pairs of electrons in each covalent bond in the diagram below.
- Which element lost an electron *to* the other? Which element gained an electron *from* the other?

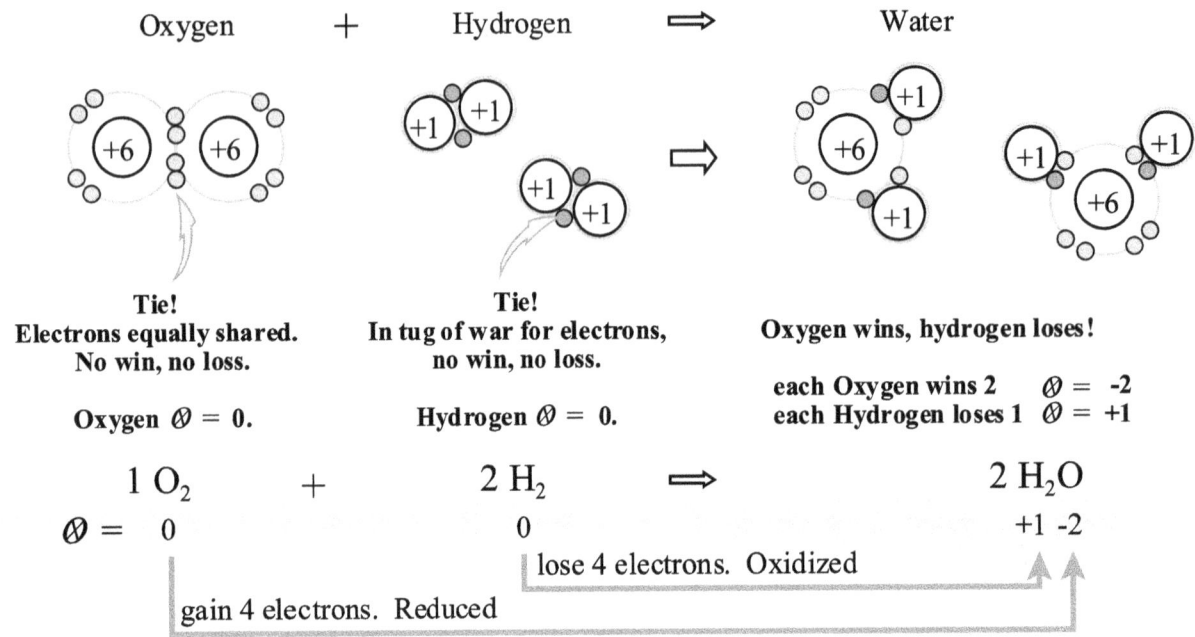

Example 2: Oxygen and hydrogen can form another compound, hydrogen peroxide.

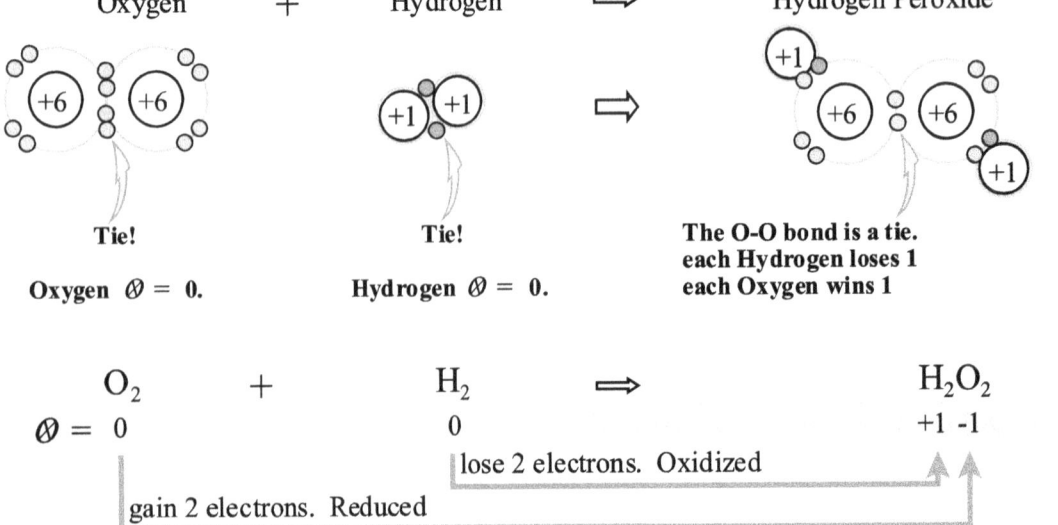

... Redox Reactions

Name:
Date:

What Are We Doing? In the two exercises below, add words, numbers and diagrams as needed to complete the diagrams like the examples on the previous page.

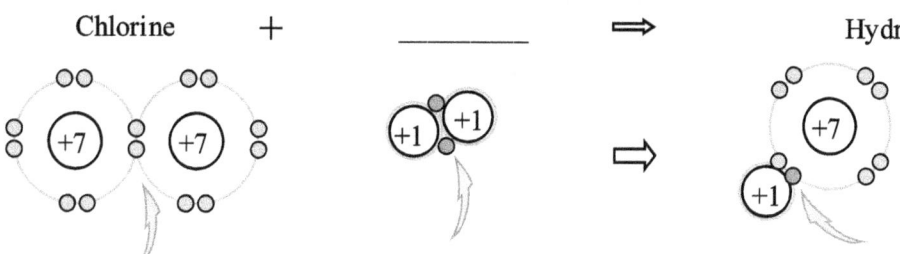

Chlorine + _____ ⇒ Hydrogen Chloride

Win, lose or tie?   Win lose or tie?   Win, lose or tie?

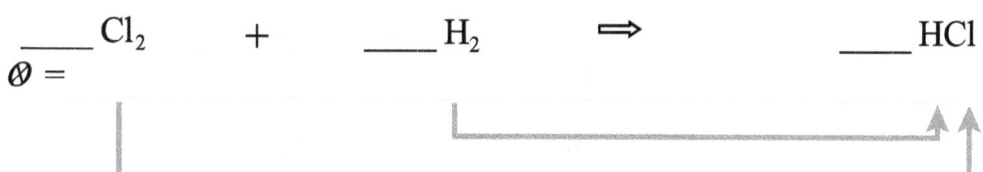

____ Cl$_2$ + ____ H$_2$ ⇒ ____ HCl

∅ =

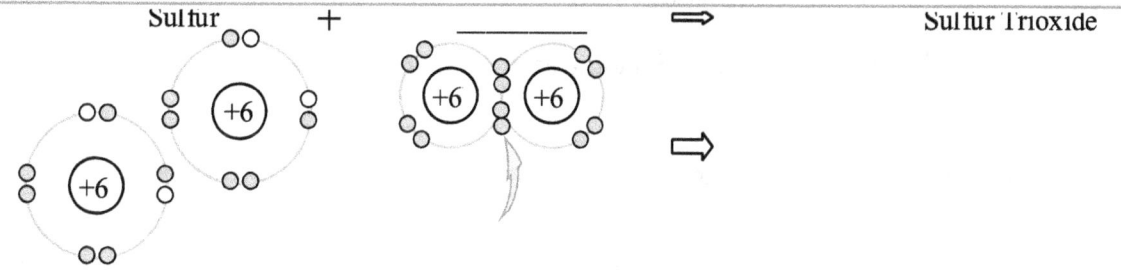

Sulfur + _____ ⇒ Sulfur Trioxide

Win lose or tie?   Win, lose or tie?

____ S + ____ O$_2$ ⇒ ____ SO$_3$

∅ =

Questions For Later...
1. Identify the substance being reduced in each case. It is known as the oxidizing agent. What are the core, valence and radius characteristics of the oxidizing agents? Explain.

© Ross Lattner Publishing   63   www.rosslattner.ca

Table Talk
Student Exercises

Covalent Molecules ...

Activity 2.4: Redox Reactions among Covalent Molecules

Do you Remember? Complete the core - valence - radius diagrams below.

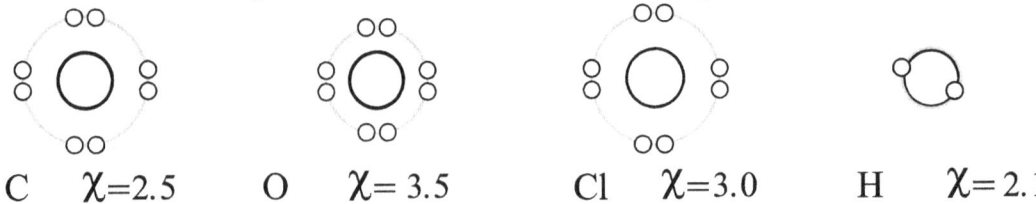

C χ=2.5   O χ=3.5   Cl χ=3.0   H χ=2.1

What's The Question? Many redox reactions involve covalent molecules. *How do we represent redox reactions among covalent molecules?* We represent them in the same way as the other reactions.

What Are We Doing? In the example below, someone has already solved the problem. Follow the next 5 steps, and circle or underline each item in the diagrams below those steps.

1. Inspect the chemical equation, and balance it by adding coefficients.

2. Study each bonding pair the Ross diagrams below. Add a small arrow to indicate electrons which have moved away from one atom and toward another.

3. Determine the ∅ for each atom. Write it below each element in the balanced equation.

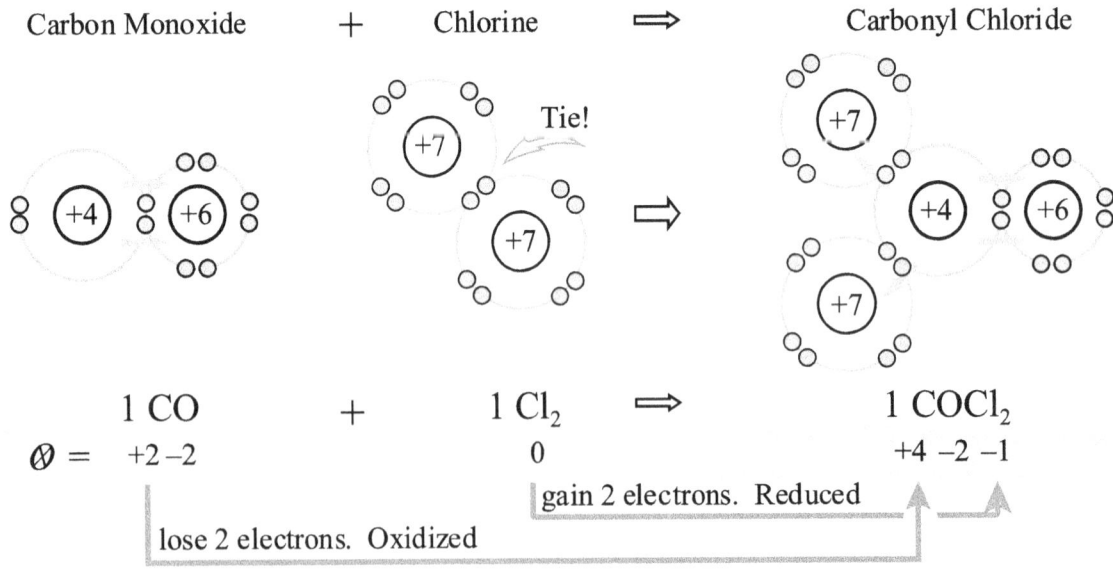

4. Determine which element(s) have had ∅ remain unchanged during the reaction.

5. Carbon began at ∅ = +4 and ended at ∅ = +2. It was reduced, that is, "gained" 2 electrons.

6. Chlorine began at ∅ = −1 and ended at ∅ = 0. Each Cl "lost" 1 electron, and was oxidized.

© Ross Lattner Publishing   www.rosslattner.ca

... Redox Reactions

Name:
Date:

What Are We Doing? In the two exercises below, add words, numbers and diagrams as needed to complete the diagrams like the examples on the previous page.

1. Hydrogen Peroxide + Hydrochloric acid ⇒ Chlorine + Water

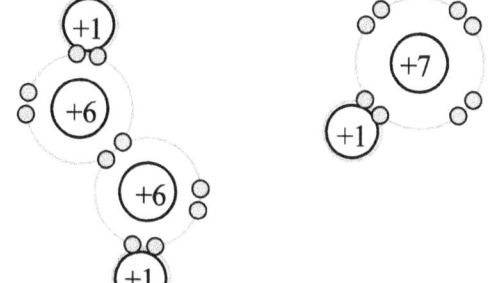

____ H₂O₂ + ____ HCl ⇒ ____ Cl₂ ____ H₂O

∅ =

2. Carbonyl Fluoride ⇒ Carbon Tetrafluoride + Carbon Dioxide

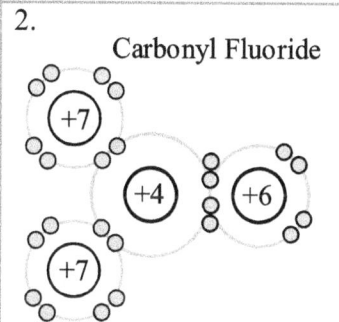 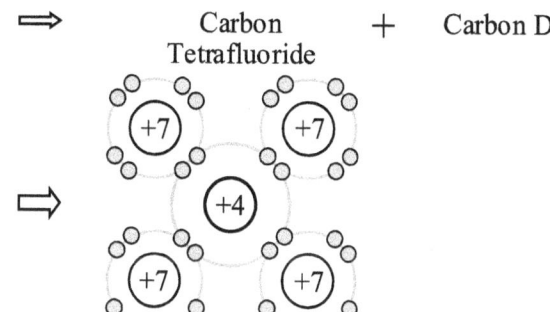

____ COF₂ ⇒ ____ CF₄ + ____ CO₂

∅ =

Questions For Later...
1. When a redox reaction occurs among covalently bonded molecules, are electrons lost or gained? Explain your answer in three or four sentences.

You can say something nice, dear, if you think long enough

How Good is your Table Talk?

Quiz 2: Redox Reactions
Add words, numbers and diagrams as needed to completely represent each reaction.

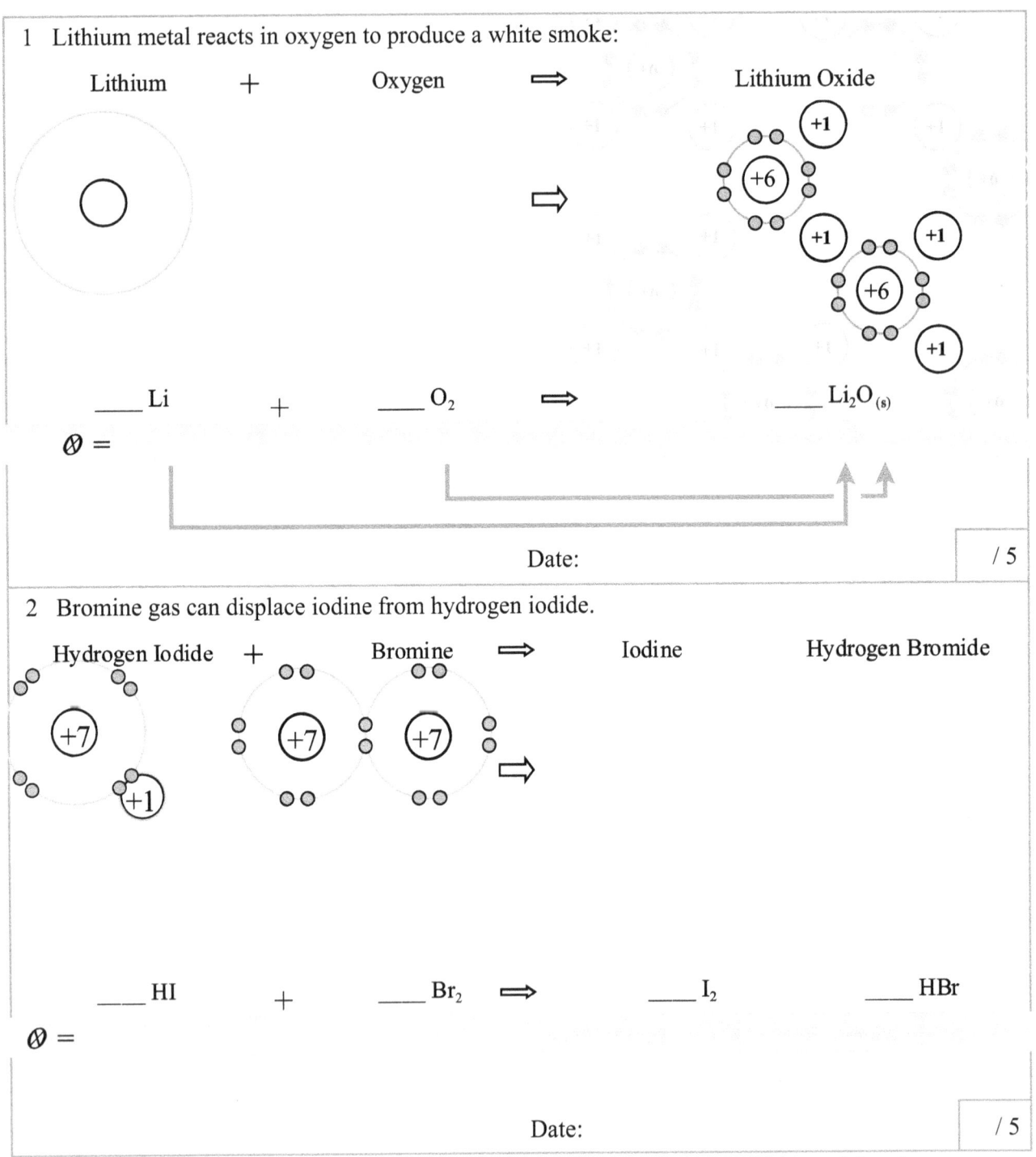

1. Lithium metal reacts in oxygen to produce a white smoke:

   Lithium + Oxygen ⇒ Lithium Oxide

   ___ Li + ___ O_2 ⇒ ___ $Li_2O_{(s)}$

   ⌀ =

   Date: ___ / 5

2. Bromine gas can displace iodine from hydrogen iodide.

   Hydrogen Iodide + Bromine ⇒ Iodine   Hydrogen Bromide

   ___ HI + ___ Br_2 ⇒ ___ I_2 ___ HBr

   ⌀ =

   Date: ___ / 5

In (1) and (2) above, who gained and who lost electrons? Use the Ross model to explain *why*.

© Ross Lattner Publishing   www.rosslattner.ca

You can say something nice, dear, if you think long enough
How Good is your Table Talk?

Quiz 2: Redox Reactions Name:

Add words, numbers and diagrams as needed to completely represent each reaction.

3 Sulfur trioxide is used to make sulfuric acid. Balance and complete this reaction:

Oxygen + Sulfur Dioxide ⇒ Sulfur Trioxide

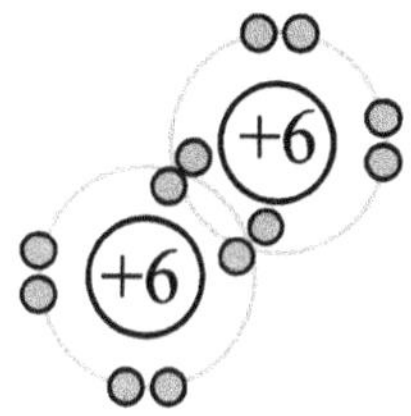

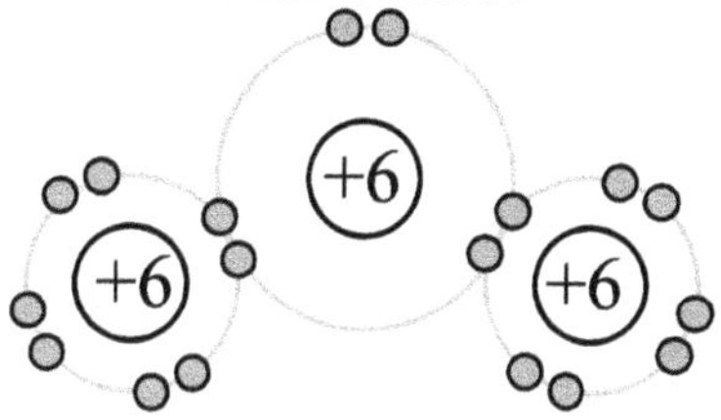

___ O₂ + ___ SO₂ ⇒ ___ SO₃

⊘ =

Date: /5

4 Magnesium metal is one of the few substances that will burn in carbon dioxide:

Magnesium + Carbon Dioxide ⇒ Carbon   Magnesium Oxide

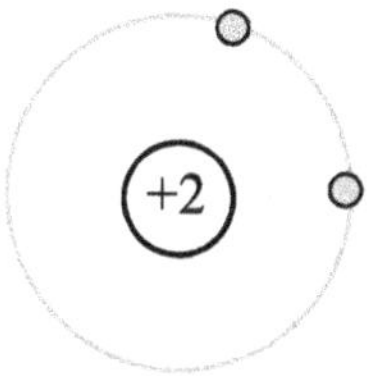

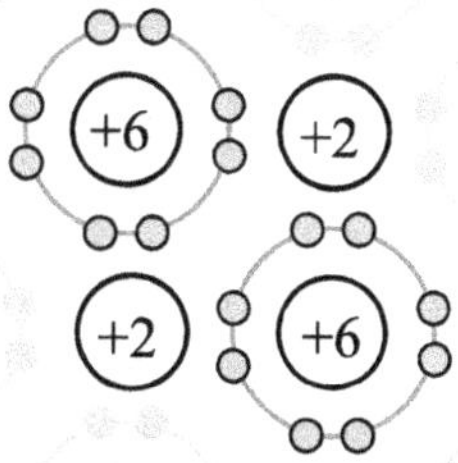

___ Mg + ___ CO₂ ⇒ ___ C   ___ MgO

⊘ =

Date: /5

In (3) and (4) above, who gained and who lost electrons? Use the Ross model to explain *why*.

© Ross Lattner Publishing   67   www.rosslattner.ca

You can say something nice, dear, if you think long enough

How Good is your Table Talk?

Quiz 2: Redox Reactions   Name:

Add words, numbers and diagrams as needed to completely represent each reaction.

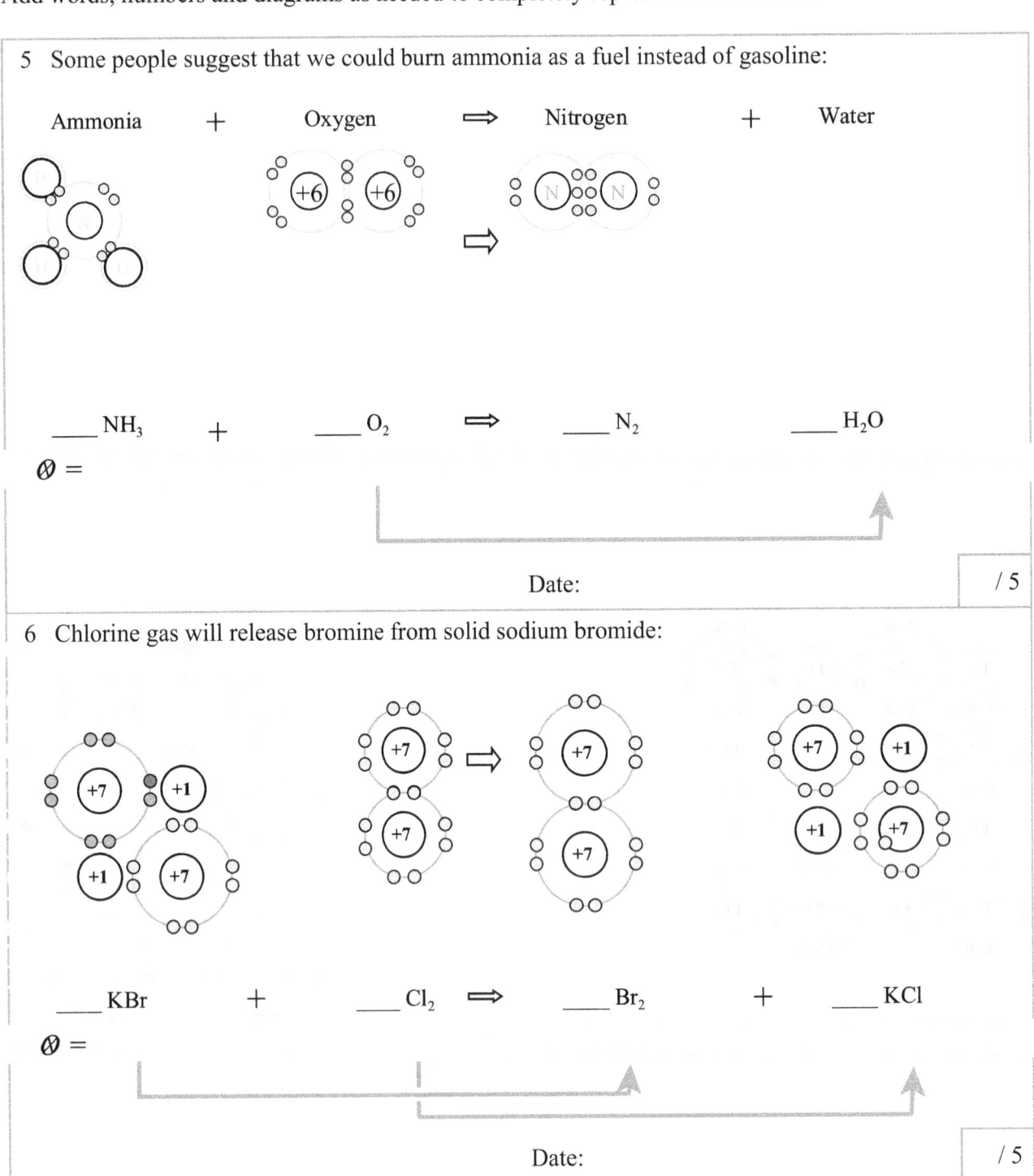

5 Some people suggest that we could burn ammonia as a fuel instead of gasoline:

   Ammonia   +   Oxygen   ⇒   Nitrogen   +   Water

   ___ NH_3 +   ___ O_2 ⇒   ___ N_2 ___ H_2O

   ⌀ =

   Date: / 5

6 Chlorine gas will release bromine from solid sodium bromide:

   ___ KBr   +   ___ Cl_2 ⇒   ___ Br_2 +   ___ KCl

   ⌀ =

   Date: / 5

In (5) and (6) above, who gained and who lost electrons? Use the Ross model to explain *why*.

You can say something nice, dear, if you think long enough

How Good is your Table Talk?

Quiz 2: Redox Reactions Name:

Add words, numbers and diagrams as needed to completely represent each reaction.

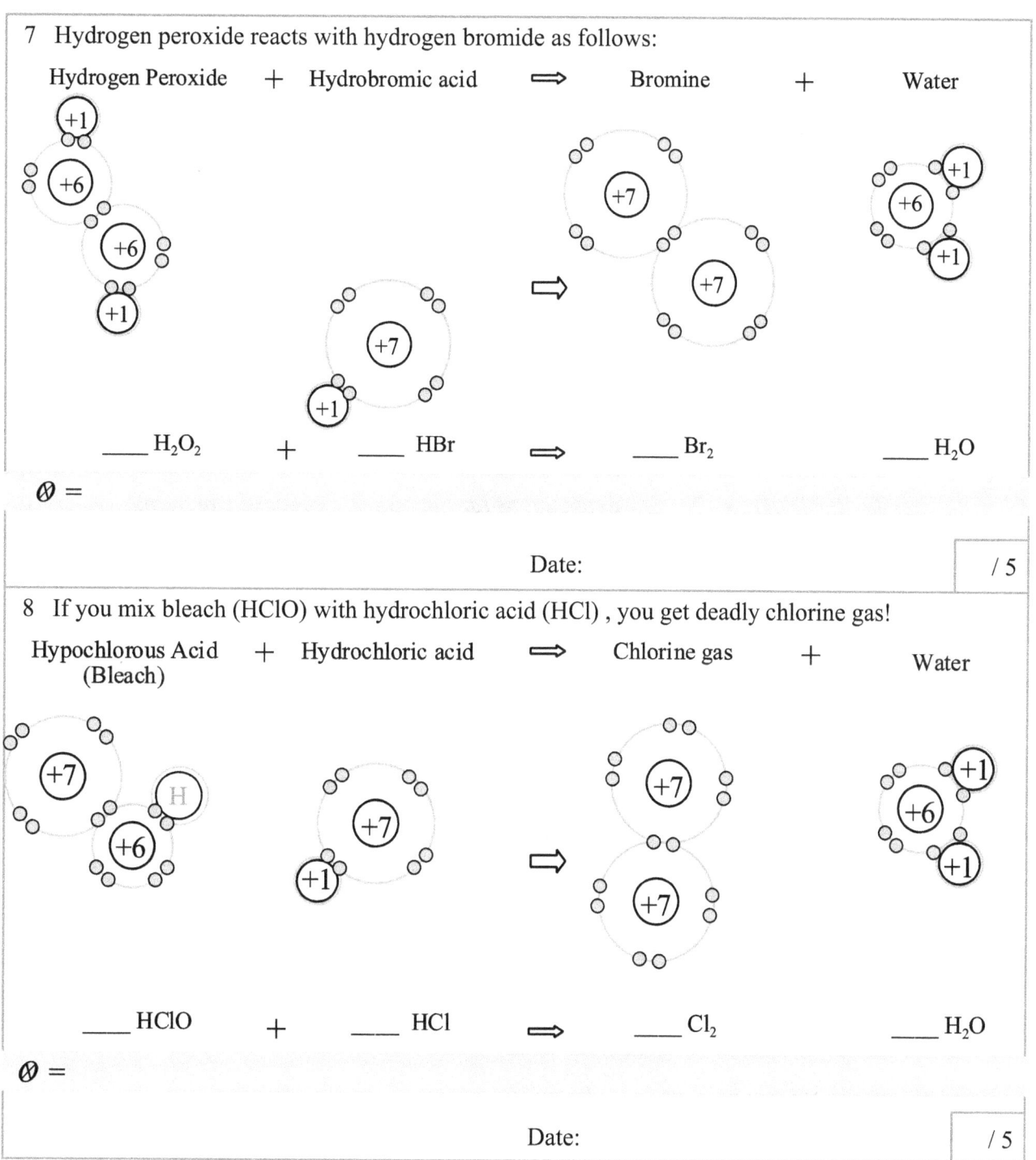

7 Hydrogen peroxide reacts with hydrogen bromide as follows:

Hydrogen Peroxide + Hydrobromic acid ⇒ Bromine + Water

___ H_2O_2 + ___ HBr ⇒ ___ Br_2 + ___ H_2O

∅ =

Date: / 5

8 If you mix bleach (HClO) with hydrochloric acid (HCl), you get deadly chlorine gas!

Hypochlorous Acid (Bleach) + Hydrochloric acid ⇒ Chlorine gas + Water

___ HClO + ___ HCl ⇒ ___ Cl_2 + ___ H_2O

∅ =

Date: / 5

In (7) and (8) above, who gained and who lost electrons? Use the Ross model to explain *why*.

Table Talk
Student Exercises

Who Gets the Electron ...

Activity 3.1: Carbon and Hydrogen

Do you Remember? Complete the core - valence - radius diagrams below.

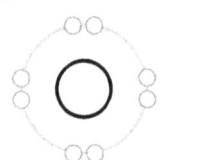  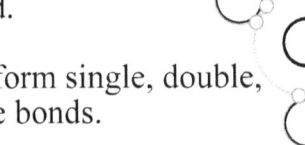 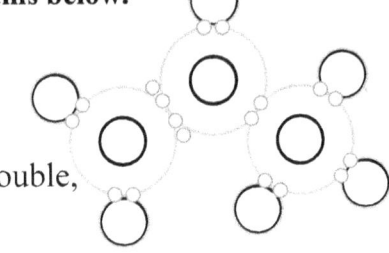

C and H can only form a single bond.

C and C can form single, double, or even triple bonds.

C $\chi = 2.5$ H $\chi = 2.1$

What Are We Thinking About?
- A hydrogen atom has only one electron to share, and can form only one covalent bond.
- Carbon has four electrons to share, and almost always forms four covalent bonds.
- Each covalent bond contains one electron from the C atom, and one from the other atom.

What's The Question? There are over three million compounds containing mostly carbon and hydrogen. That's many times more compounds than all of the other elements combined. To keep track of them, chemists use *simplified structural diagrams* to represent organic molecules. *How do we read a simplified structural diagram of an organic molecule?*

Core Valence Radius Diagrams	*Conventions for Simplified Structural Diagrams*
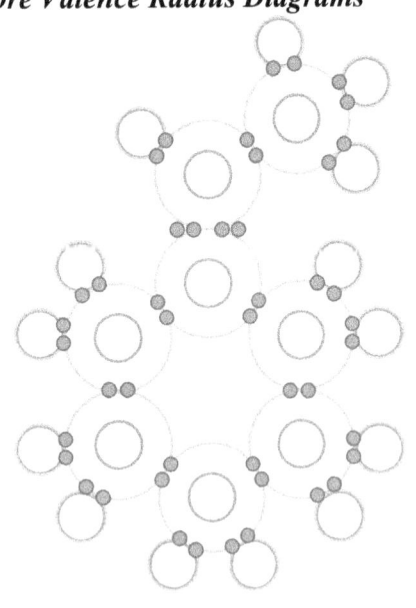	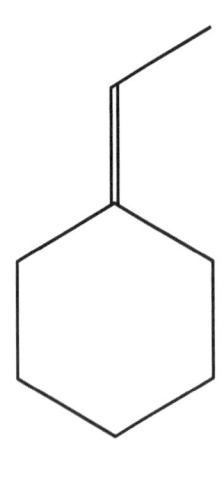

The diagrams above both depict the same compound!

1. Find all of the carbon atoms in the molecule above left. For each C-C bond, connect the cores with a straight line. You have just drawn the simplified structural diagram!

2. Examine the simplified structural diagram above right. Each vertex (corner or end) is a carbon atom. Since carbon always forms four bonds, you can figure out how many hydrogens are attached to each vertex. Draw them in lightly with a pencil.

© Ross Lattner Publishing   www.rosslattner.ca

... Organic Molecules

Name:
Date:

What Are We Doing? Each box should contain one Ross diagram and one simplified structural diagram. In each box, one of the diagrams is missing. Draw the matching diagram for each molecule.

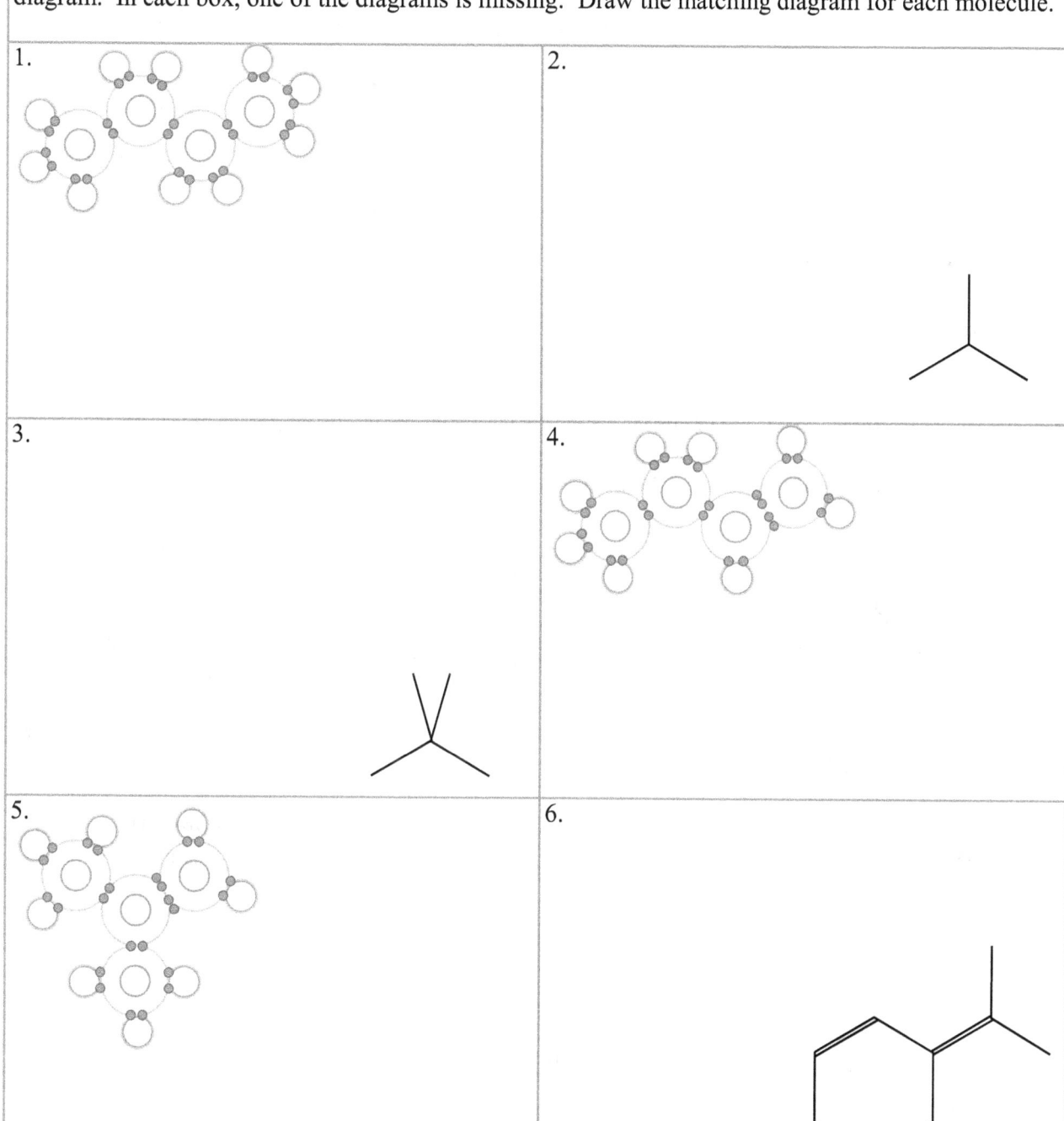

Questions For Later...

1. Choose any three of the simplified structural diagrams. Draw a small circle around each vertex. How many bonds will that circle cut? Explain.

Table Talk
Student Exercises

Who Loses Electrons ...

Activity 3.2: Oxidation Numbers in Hydrocarbons

Do you Remember? Complete the core - valence - radius diagrams below.

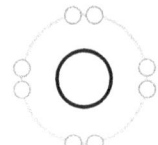 

C and H do not share electrons equally. Who wins, who loses?

C and C share electrons equally...

C $\chi = 2.5$ H $\chi = 2.1$ A tie!! No one wins, no one loses.

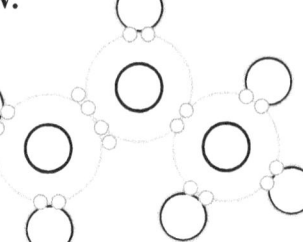

What Are We Thinking About?
- Carbon's core charge is greater, increasing carbon's attraction for electrons.
- Hydrogen's radius is smallest, also increasing hydrogen's attraction for electrons.
- The electronegativities are similar, but carbon is slightly more attractive to electrons.

What's The Question? In a C - H bond, the electrons are almost equally shared. Hydrogen's electrons, move slightly toward the carbon atom. That slight movement is counted as oxidation of the hydrogen, and reduction of the carbon. *What are the oxidation numbers in hydrocarbon molecules?*

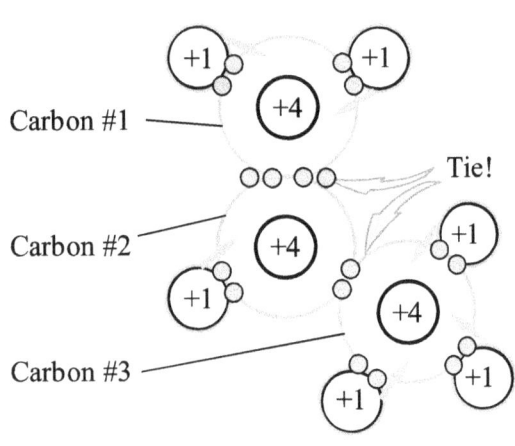

What Are We Doing? We find the oxidation number of each carbon the same way as all covalent molecules.

Hydrogen   will always "lose" its only electron to C. H is always assigned ⊘ = +1

Carbon #1   has "won" two electrons, and tied two. It is assigned ⊘ = –2.

Carbon #2   has "won" one electron from H, and tied 3 with the carbons. It is assigned ⊘ = –1.

Carbon #3   has "won" three electrons from the H atoms. It is assigned ⊘ = –3.

Here is same molecule in a simplified structural diagram. First, we draw a light circle around each vertex.

Carbon #1   two CC bonds means tie for two. There must be two H atoms, so ⊘ = –2.

Carbon #2   the circle cuts three CC bonds. Only one H bonded here, so ⊘ = –1

Carbon #3   the circle cuts only 1 CC bond, so there are three CH bonds. ⊘ = –3

© Ross Lattner Publishing   www.rosslattner.ca

... Organic Molecules

Name:
Date:

What Are We Doing? Find the oxidation number for each carbon in every molecule below.

1. 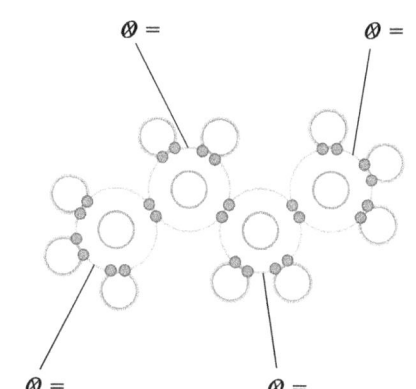	2. Ø = Ø = Ø = Ø =
3. 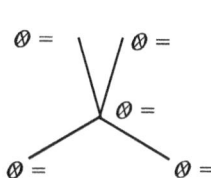	4. 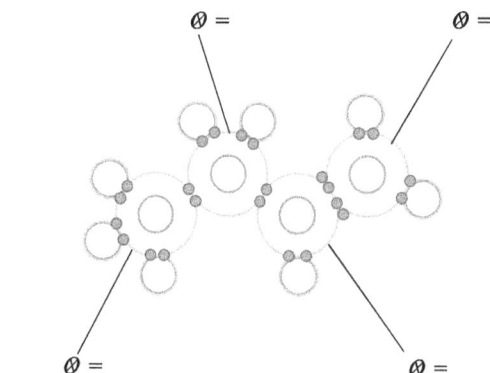
5. 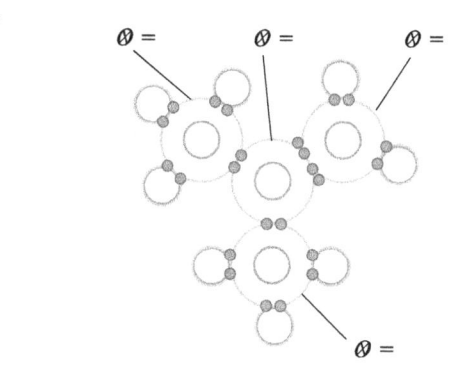	6. Ø = Ø = Ø = Ø = Ø = Ø = Ø = Ø = Ø =

Questions For Later...

1. What are the possible values for the oxidation numbers of carbon in hydrocarbon molecules? Explain.

2. There are two different molecules with the chemical formula C_4H_{10}. Can you deduce the oxidation numbers of the carbon in those molecules from the chemical formula? Explain.

Table Talk
Student Exercises

When you have more than one ...

Activity 3.3: Oxygen and Nitrogen in Organic Molecules

Do you Remember? Complete the core - valence - radius diagrams below.

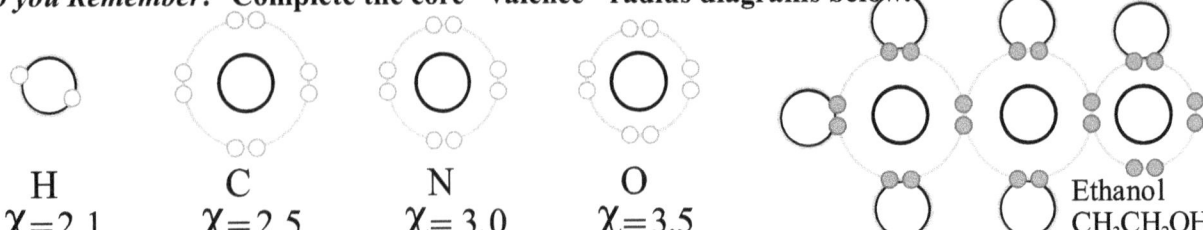

H   C   N   O
χ=2.1   χ=2.5   χ=3.0   χ=3.5   Ethanol
                                                    CH_3CH_2OH

What Are We Thinking About?
- Oxygen and nitrogen can be included in organic molecules.
- Oxygen forms two covalent bonds, and N usually forms three covalent bonds with C and H.
- Nitrogen, ε = 3.0, can attract electrons more strongly than carbon.
- Oxygen, ε = 3.5, is can attract electrons from H, C, and N.

What's The Question? Nitrogen or oxygen in an organic molecule can greatly affect the oxidation number of the carbon atoms in the molecule. *What are the oxidation numbers in organic molecules containing C, H, N and O?*

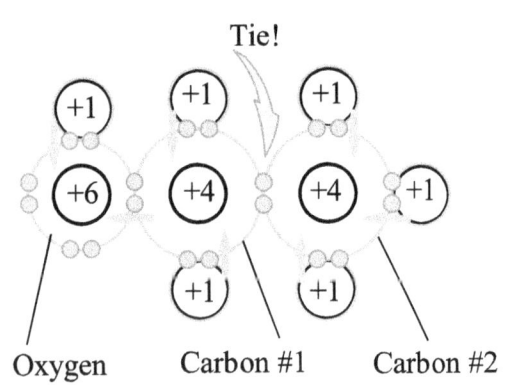

Oxygen   Carbon #1   Carbon #2

What Are We Doing?	Find ∅ for each atom in ethanol.
Hydrogen	the big "loser." H always has ∅ = +1
Oxygen	the big "winner." always has ∅ = −2.
Carbon #1	"wins" three from the hydrogens, ties one with carbon. It is assigned ∅ = −3.
Carbon #2	"wins" two, "loses" one to oxygen, and ties one with carbon. It is assigned ∅ = −1.

Here is the simplified structural diagram. Daw a light circle around each vertex.

H-O
  \
   _/\
   / \
  /   \

Oxygen   Carbon #1   Carbon #2

Oxygen	the circle cuts two bonds, and oxygen always wins, so ∅ = −2.
Carbon #1	the circle cuts one CC bonds (tie) and one CO bond (lose). There must be two H atoms bonded here, so ∅ = −1
Carbon #3	one CC bond, three CH bonds, so ∅ = −3.

© Ross Lattner Publishing   www.rosslattner.ca

... Organic Molecules

Name:
Date:

What Are We Doing? Find the oxidation number for each carbon in every molecule below.

1. Methanol, CH_3OH 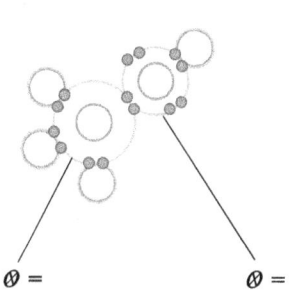 ⊘ = ⊘ =	2. Propanone (Acetone) CH_3COCH_3 ⊘ = O ⊘ = ⊘ = ⊘ =
3. Ethanoic acid, (acetic acid) CH_3COOH ⊘ = ⊘ = ⊘ = ⊘ = ⊘ = O H ⊘ = O ⊘ =	4. Diethyl ether $C_2H_5OC_2H_5$ ⊘ = O ⊘ = ⊘ = ⊘ = ⊘ =
5. Glutamine, an amino acid O HO — — NH$_2$ NH$_2$ O	6. Glycerine, a sugar-like molecule used in candy. 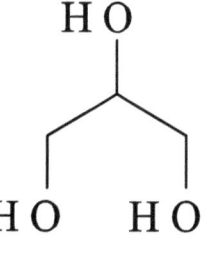HO HO HO

Questions For Later...

1. What is a "carboxyl group?" Look it up, and find the carboxyl groups in the molecules above.

2. Look up "carbonyl group" and find carbonyl groups in the molecules above.

3. The molecules above contain the functional groups: alcohols, amines, carboxylic acids, ethers and ketones. Look these groups up, then name them in the molecules above.

Table Talk
Student Exercises

Redox Reactions of ...

Activity 3.4: Redox Reactions of Organic Molecules

Do you Remember? Complete the core - valence - radius diagrams below.

H	C	N	O
$\chi = 2.1$	$\chi = 2.5$	$\chi = 3.0$	$\chi = 3.5$

What's The Question? The redox reactions of organic molecules is of great interest in biochemistry. For example, metabolism involves hundreds of different redox reactions.

What Are We Doing? In the example below, someone has already solved the problem. Follow the next 5 steps, and circle or underline each item in the diagrams below those steps.

1. Inspect the chemical equation, and balance it by adding coefficients.
2. Study each diagram. Add a small arrow to indicate an electron which has moved away from one atom and toward another.
3. Determine the ⊘ for each atom. Write it below each element in the balanced equation.

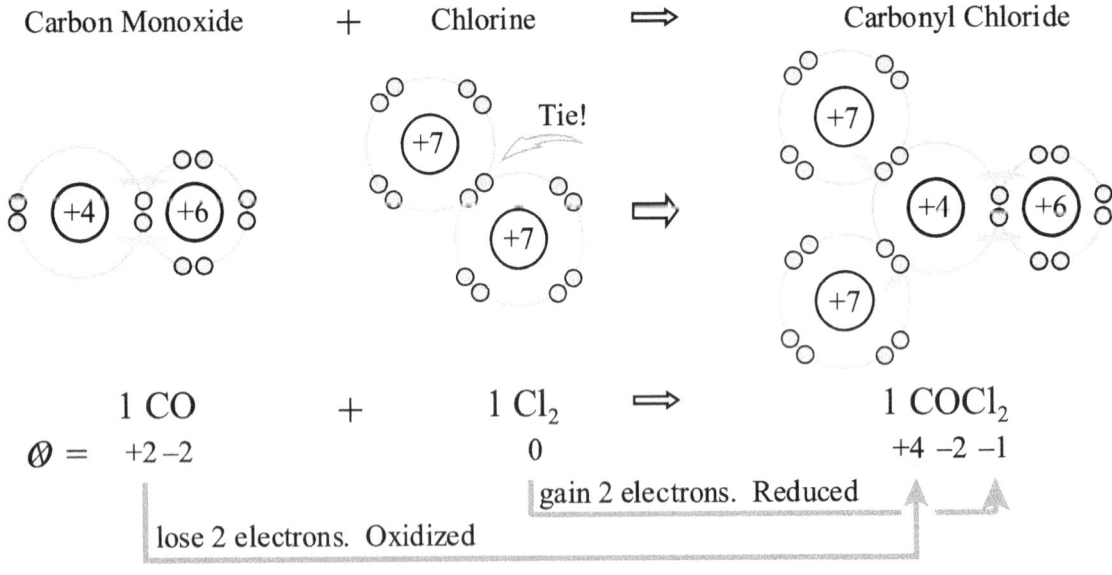

Carbon Monoxide	+	Chlorine	⟹	Carbonyl Chloride
1 CO	+	1 Cl$_2$	⟹	1 COCl$_2$
⊘ = +2 −2		0		+4 −2 −1

lose 2 electrons. Oxidized

gain 2 electrons. Reduced

4. Determine which atom(s) have had ⊘ remain unchanged during the reaction.

5. Carbon began at ⊘ = +2 and ended at ⊘ = +4. It was oxidized, that is, "lost" 2 electrons.

6. Chlorine began at ⊘ = 0 and ended at ⊘ = −1. Each Cl "gained" 1 electron, and was reduced.

... Organic Molecules

Name:
Date:

1. A strong oxidizer such a chromate ion oxidize 1 propanol, to propanal. The oxidation half-reaction is shown below. Complete the diagrams by adding words, numbers and oxidation states as required. Can you balance the redox reaction below the diagrams?

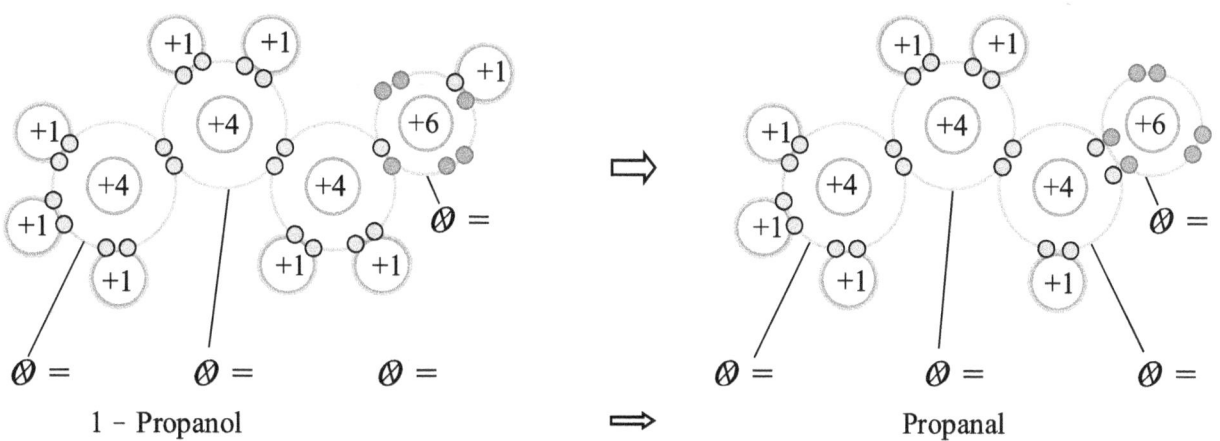

1 - Propanol ⟹ Propanal

$$CH_3CH_2CH_2OH + CrO_4^{2-} \Longrightarrow CH_3CH_2CHO + Cr^{3+}$$

2. Chromate can also oxidize 2-propanol. This time, the product is propanone. The oxidation half-reaction is shown below. Complete the diagrams by adding words, numbers and oxidation states as required. Balance the redox reaction below the diagrams.

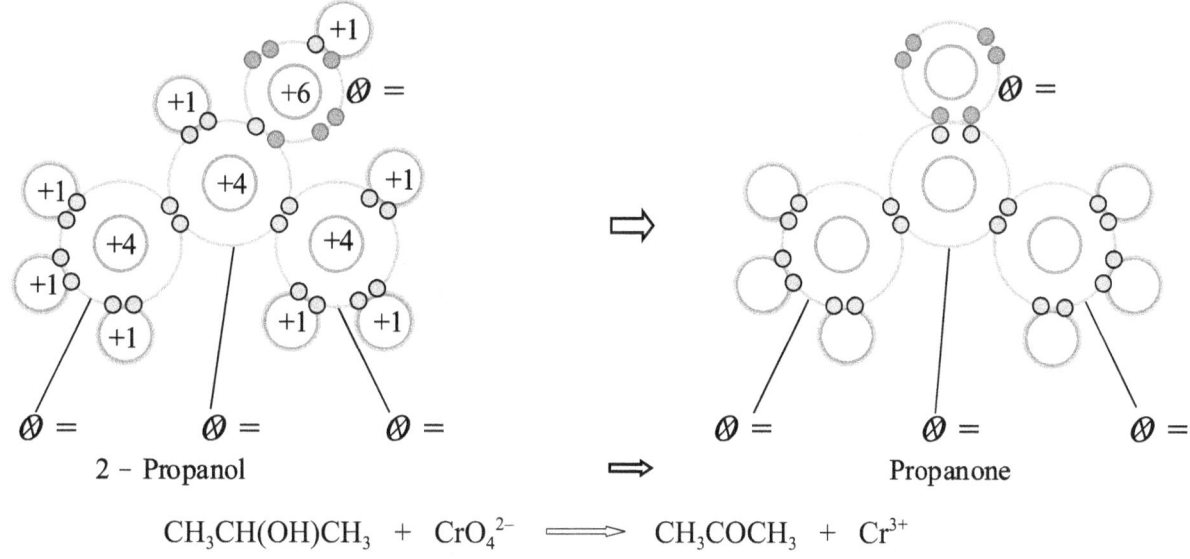

2 - Propanol ⟹ Propanone

$$CH_3CH(OH)CH_3 + CrO_4^{2-} \Longrightarrow CH_3COCH_3 + Cr^{3+}$$

Questions For Later...
1. When a redox reaction occurs among covalently bonded molecules, are electrons lost or gained? Explain your answer in three or four sentences.

You can say something nice, dear, if you think long enough

How Good is your Table Talk?

Quiz 3: Oxidation and Reduction in Organic Chemistry

1 Formaldehyde H₂CO, is a toxic material found in plastics. Find ⌀ of each element.

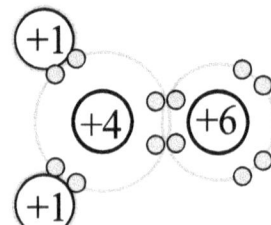

Date: _____ / 5

2 Hydrogen cyanide is another extremely toxic gas. It can be formed in house fires from burning wool. Find ⌀ of each element.

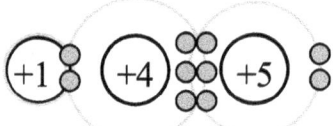

Date: _____ / 5

3 When natural gas burns with insufficient air, it can produce toxic formaldehyde.

    Methane   +   Oxygen   ⇒   Formaldehyde   Water

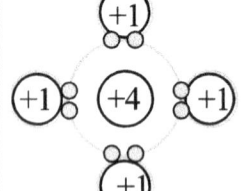   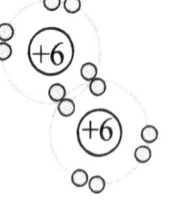 ⇒ 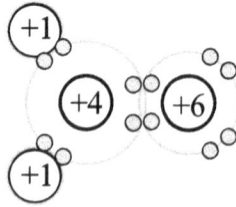

___ CH₄   +   ___ O₂ ⇒ ___ H₂CO   ___ H₂O

⌀ =

Date: _____ / 5

You can say something nice, dear, if you think long enough
How Good is your Table Talk?

Quiz 3: Oxidation and Reduction in Organic Chemistry   Name:

4   Benzene is a potent carcinogen. Avoid all contact. Find Ø of each element. Don't forget that the hydrogen atoms are not shown in a simplified structural diagram!

5   Purine is the basis of many life processes. Find Ø of each element. Once again, be sure to count the hydrogens that are actually present, but left out of this diagram.

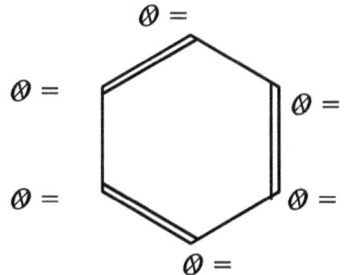

Date: / 5   Date: / 5

6   Acetylene gas is produced by reacting calcium carbide with water in the reaction:

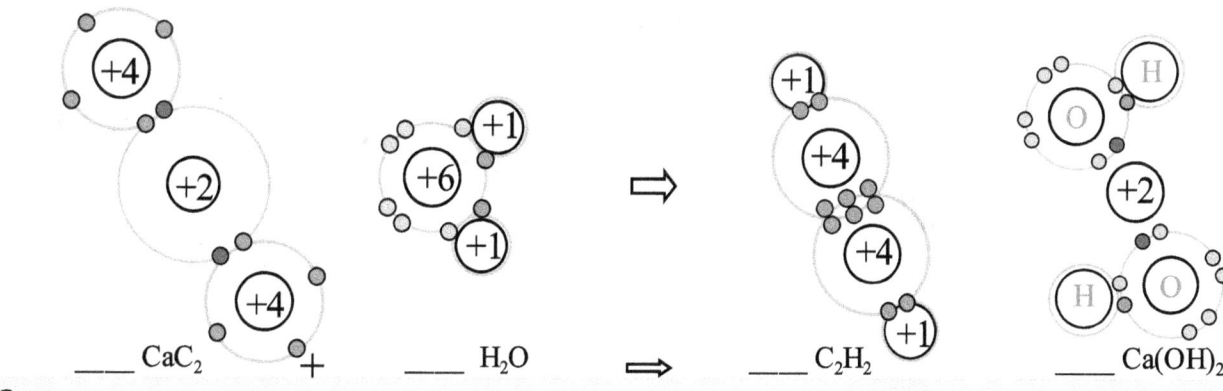

___ CaC_2 + ___ H_2O ⇒ ___ C_2H_2 ___ $Ca(OH)_2$

Ø =

Date: / 5

You can say something nice, dear, if you think long enough

How Good is your Table Talk?

Quiz 3: Oxidation and Reduction in Organic Chemistry   Name:

7   Methyl imine is thought to be a precursor of life on earth. It is also found in the gas between stars, and in distant galaxies. Find ∅ of each element.

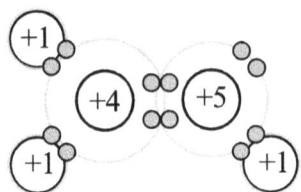

8   Crown ethers are hydrocarbon rings containing oxygen. They might become valuable ionic filters in the future. Find ∅ of each element.

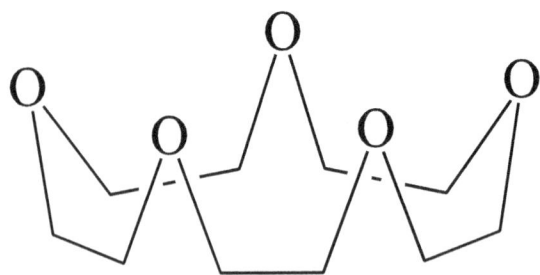

Date: / 5   Date: / 5

9   Photosynthesis provides almost all biological energy on the planet. Complete and balance this diagram, and find the changes in oxidation number in carbon and oxygen.

Carbon Dioxide   +   Water   ⟹   Glucose   +   Oxygen

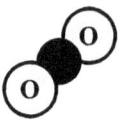 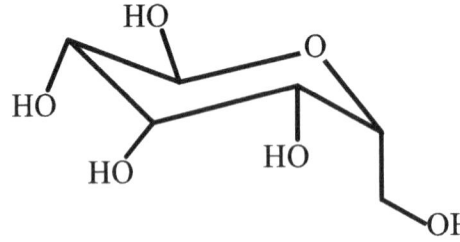

___ CO_2 +   ___ H_2O ⟹   ___ $C_6H_{12}O_6$ +   ___ O_2

∅ =

Date: / 5

© Ross Lattner Publishing   80   www.rosslattner.ca

You can say something nice, dear, if you think long enough

How Good is your Table Talk?

Quiz 3: Oxidation and Reduction in Organic Chemistry   Name:

---

10 Our bodies can't make the amino acid methionine. We must obtain it from food (beans, spinach, oranges) Find ∅ of each element.

11 Methyl - ethyl - ketone peroxide is used to start polymerization chain reactions in many plastics. Find ∅ of each element.

Date: _____   / 5   Date: _____   / 5

12 Dinitroethane can decompose rapidly, in a devastating explosion. Is this a redox reaction?

Dinitroethane ⇒ Carbon Monoxide + Nitrogen + Water

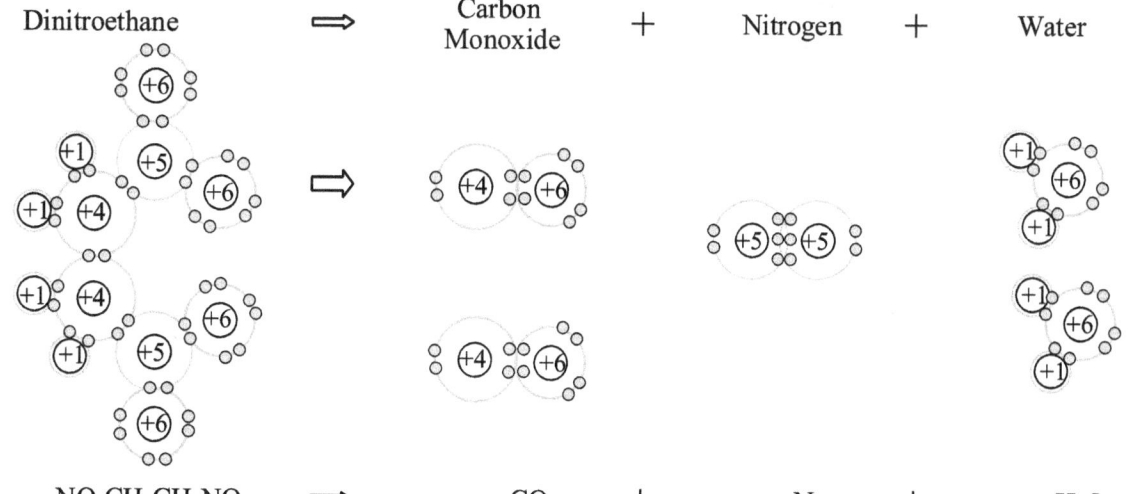

___ $NO_2CH_2CH_2NO_2$ ⇒ ___ CO + ___ N_2 + ___ H_2O

Date: _____   / 5

Table Talk
Student Exercises

Electrons and Energy ...

Activity 4.1: Electron Potential Energy

What Are We Thinking About? Take a look at the smooth, curvy funnel shape below left. We use that funnel to represent a "potential energy well," a kind of trap that electrons can "fall" into. Every positive atomic core creates a potential energy well like that, with the core at the "bottom" of the trap.

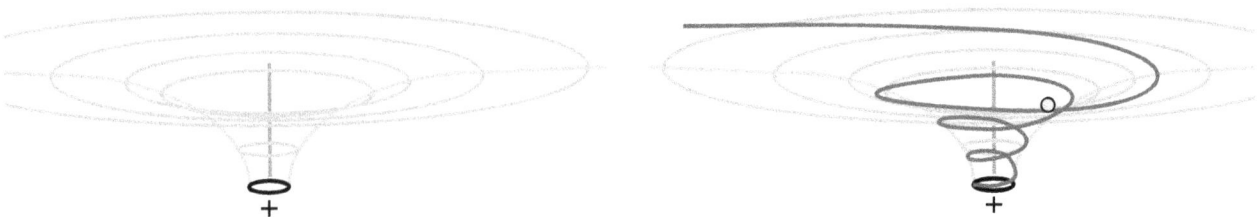

In the diagram above right, an electron has wandered close to the potential energy well. It spirals inward and "downward," faster and faster. Its potential energy is converted into kinetic and electro-magnetic energy. The closer the electron is to the core, the farther down the potential energy well it is.

What's The Question? How can we estimate the relative potential energy of electrons?

What Are We Doing? Study each example to see how core charge and radius affect the potential energy of the valence electrons.

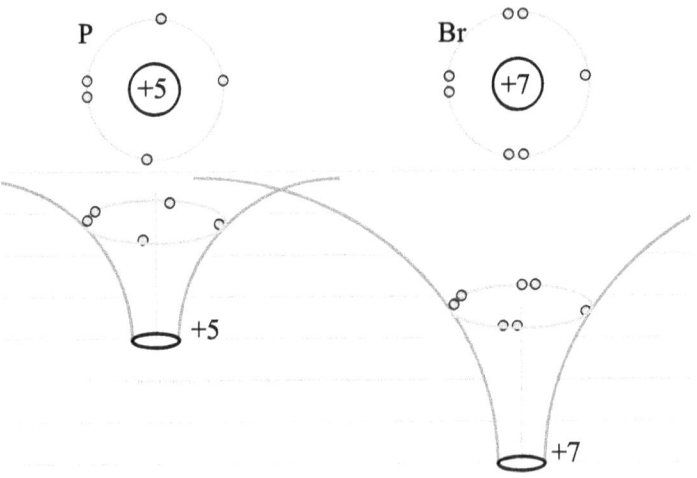

Phosphorus and bromine have the same radius

Because bromine's core charge is greater, its potential well is deeper.

Bromine's valence electrons are at a lower potential energy.

Fluorine and bromine have the same core charge, so their potential energy wells are similar in size and shape.

Because fluorine's radius is so small, the electrons are farther down in the potential energy well.

Fluorine's valence electrons are at lower potential energy than bromine's.

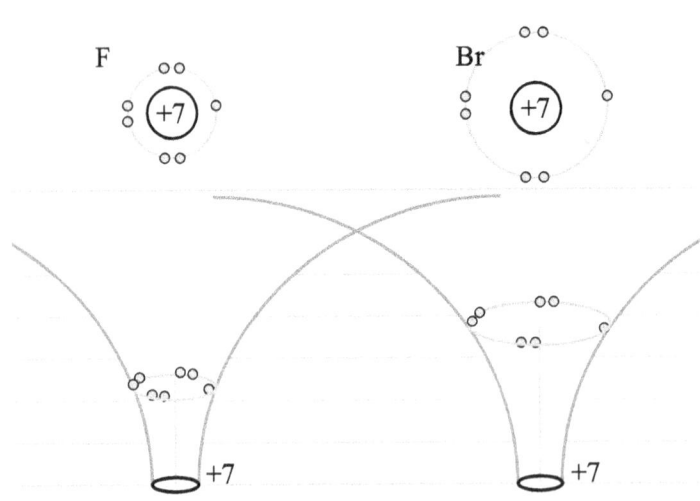

..."Falling" Towards the Core

Name:
Date:

Focus Question: Complete each of the drawings below to show the core charge, valence radius, the potential energy well and the energy level of the valence electrons.

1 Draw the valence electrons for lithium and oxygen at the matching radius in both cases.

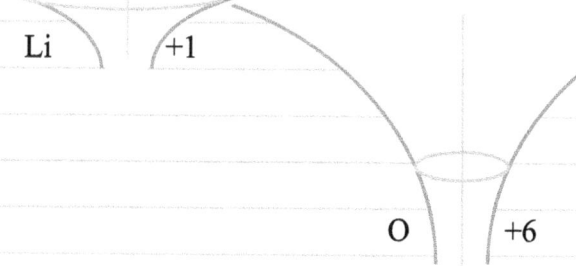

Which electrons are lower in potential energy?

2 Carbon and silicon have the same core charge, but very different chemical properties. Carbon is a non-metal, and silicon is a metalloid.

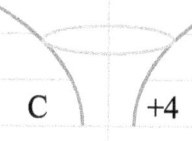

Why is Si more metallic than C?

3 Organic chemistry is based upon carbon and hydrogen. Complete the Ross and potential energy diagrams for C and H.

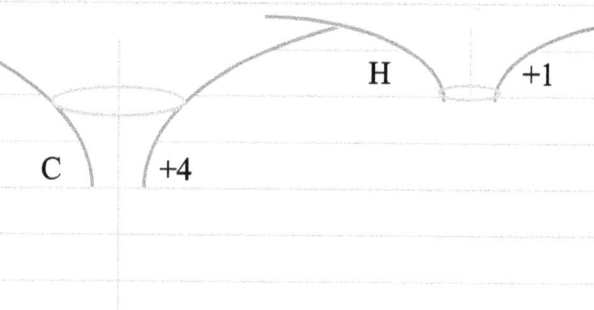

Would C-H bonds be very polar? Explain.

4 Draw potential wells for aluminum and chlorine. Place the valence electrons at the appropriate level

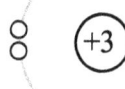 

Would chlorine be able to take an electron from aluminum?

© Ross Lattner Publishing   83   www.rosslattner.ca

Table Talk
Student Exercises

Electrons and Energy ...

Activity 4.2: The Combustion of Non-Metals

What Are We Thinking About?
- The closer an electron gets to an atomic core, the lower its potential energy. Oxygen's radius is less than sulfur's. An electron in sulfur's valence can "roll downhill" to a lower potential energy in oxygen's valence shell.
- Oxygen has both a greater core charge and a smaller radius than carbon. Oxygen's valence electrons are at a lower energy level than carbon's. When carbon and oxygen combine chemically, the electrons in carbon's valence can "roll downhill" to a lower potential energy in oxygen's valence shell.

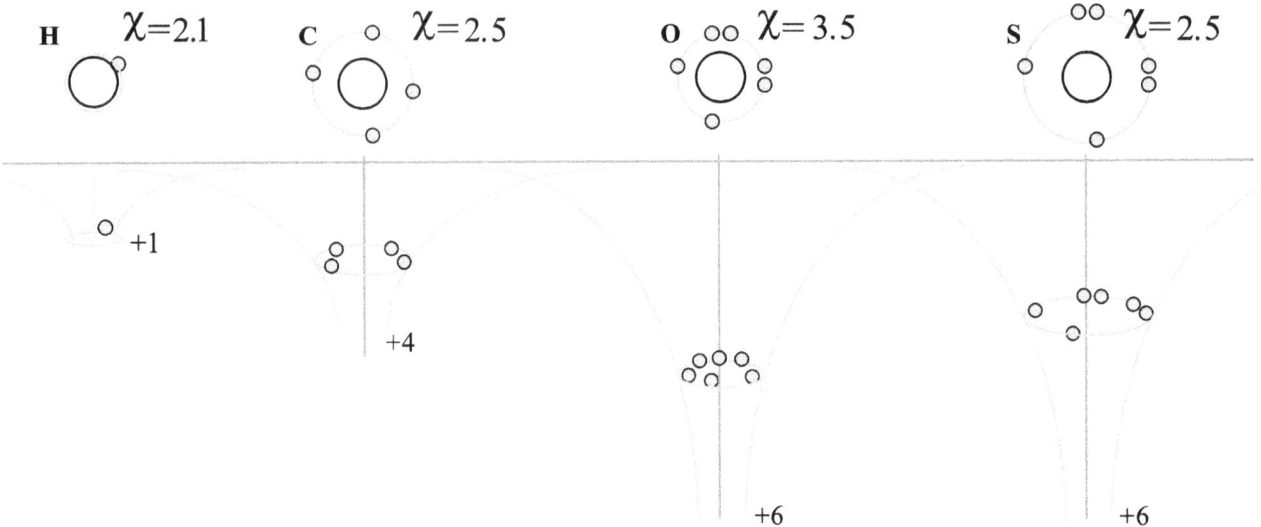

What's The Question? Every day, most of us obtain some energy from the reactions of non-metals. Perhaps we might strike a match, burn natural gas or light a candle. Let's take as our example the burning of hydrogen in oxygen. *Where does the energy of burning hydrogen come from?*

What Are We Doing? In the top part of the diagram, looking "down the throat" of the energy funnels, we see the core valence radius diagrams. Hydrogen's electron appears to be making a short hop from hydrogen toward the valence shell of oxygen.

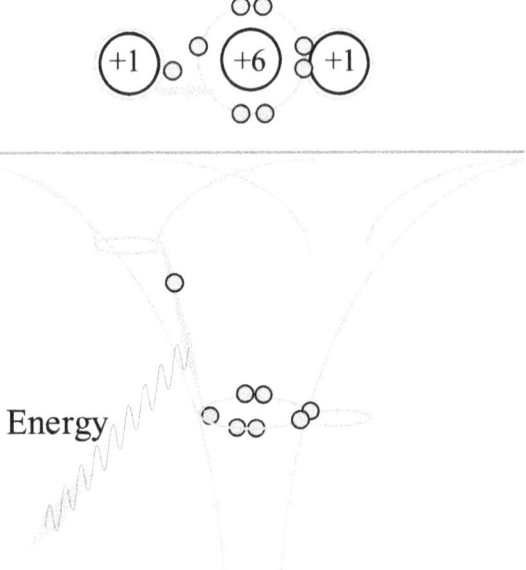

Seen from the "side," the same electron is actually making a very big drop into a deep potential energy well.

It is this loss of electron potential energy that gives off the energy when hydrogen and oxygen react to form water.

The energy comes from electrons "rolling downhill" to a lower potential energy level!

© Ross Lattner Publishing   www.rosslattner.ca

..."Falling" Towards the Core

Name:
Date:

Focus Question: Complete each of the drawings below to show core charge, valence, radius, the potential energy well and the energy level of the valence electrons. In addition, show the electron "falling" from one valence to another as the atoms approach.

1 Sulfur's electrons are about to fall more deeply into oxygen's potential well.	2 As charcoal burns, it forms carbon dioxide. All four of carbon's electrons fall more deeply into oxygen's potential well.

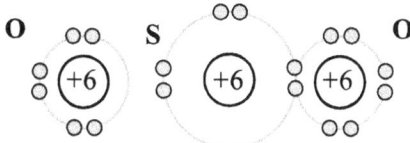
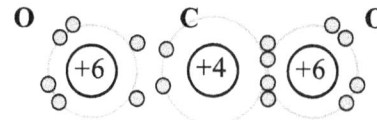

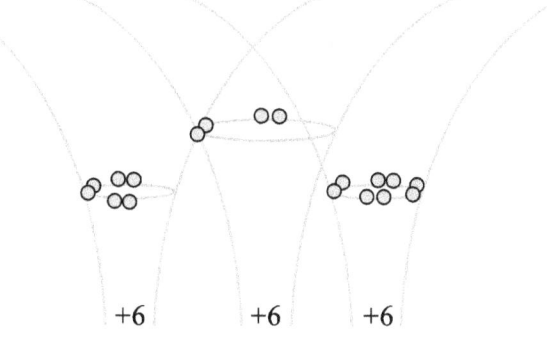
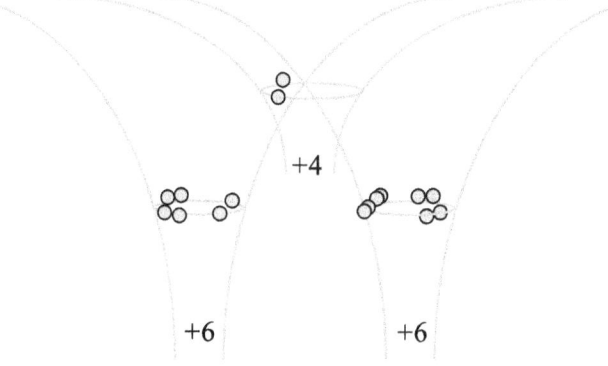

3	Which reaction would release more energy: burning sulfur, or burning carbon? Why?

4 Hydrogen sulfide is the stinky gas given off by swamps and rotten eggs. Chemically, it is similar to water.	5 Draw a potential well for chlorine. Show how hydrogen's electrons must move to form hydrogen chloride HCl.

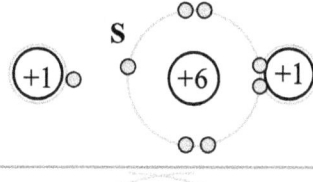
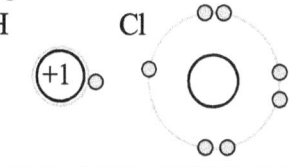

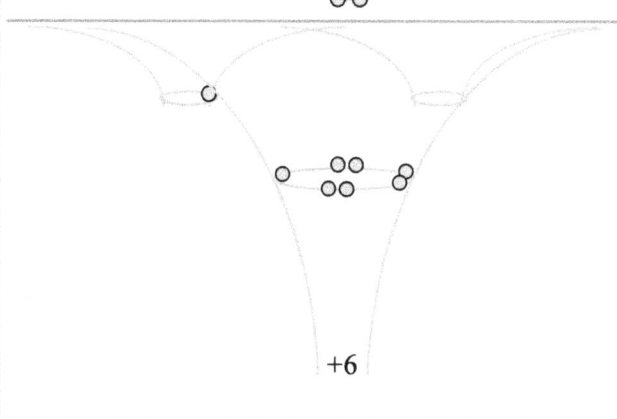

© Ross Lattner Publishing   85   www.rosslattner.ca

Table Talk
Student Exercises

Electrons and Energy ...

Activity 4.3: The Spectacular Combustion of Metals

What Are We Thinking About?
- Because of their small core charges, Mg and Na have both shallow potential wells and large radii.
- The valence electrons in Mg and Na are very high in potential energy, relative to O and S.
- Metals have valence electrons with high potential energy. In non-metals, the valence electrons are in a deep potential well. Non-metal valence electrons have low potential energy.

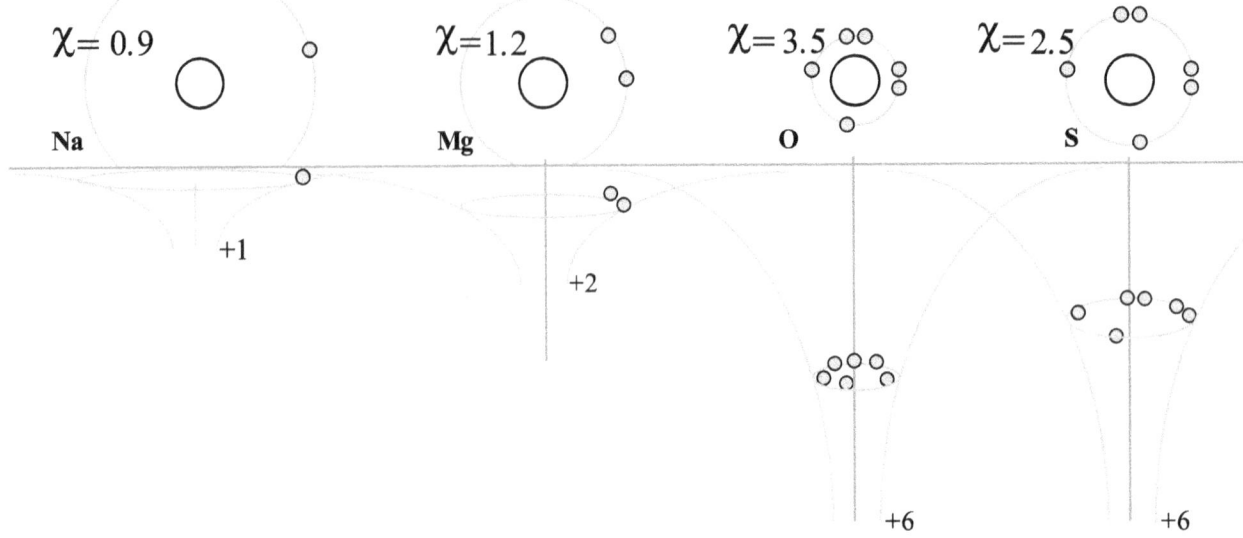

What's The Question? The combustion of magnesium is one of the most intriguing reactions in introductory chemistry. The flame, the smoke and the resulting ash are all white hot, indicating that an extraordinary amount of energy is being released. *From where does all of that energy come?*

What Are We Doing? Looking down the energy well, we see the core valence radius view. Magnesium has two loosely held electrons which move readily into Oxygen's valence, where they are closer to the +6 core charge.

Seen from the "side," magnesium's valence electrons fall deeply into oxygen's potential energy well. The electrons lose a great deal of potential energy as they fall into the well. The energy is released as heat.

But there's more! Once oxygen has custody of the electrons, two ions are formed: Mg^{2+} and O^{2-}. The Mg ion is much smaller than the original Mg atom.

The ions are able to attract each other so closely that *all* of the charges are closer together than they could have been as elements. This crystal lattice energy also adds to the heat released in the combustion of magnesium.

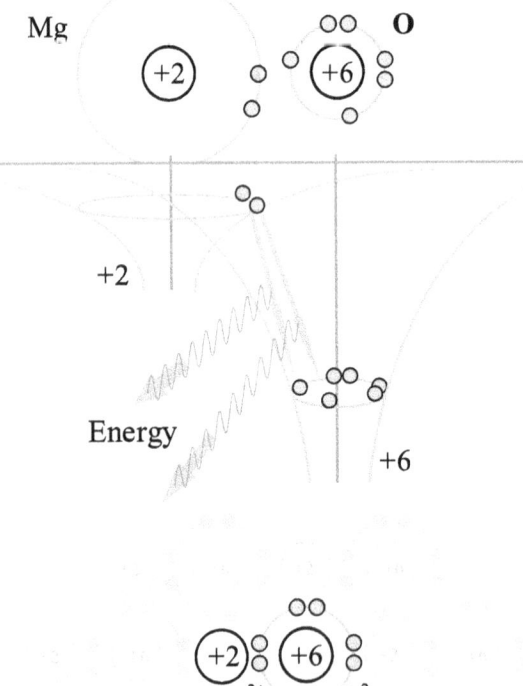

© Ross Lattner Publishing   www.rosslattner.ca

..."Falling" Towards the Core

Name:
Date:

Focus Question: Complete each of the drawings below to show core charge, valence, radius, the potential energy well and the energy level of the valence electrons. In addition, show the electrons "falling" from one valence to another as the atoms approach. Finally, draw the new crystal lattice.

1. Sodium burns with a bright yellow flame in oxygen.

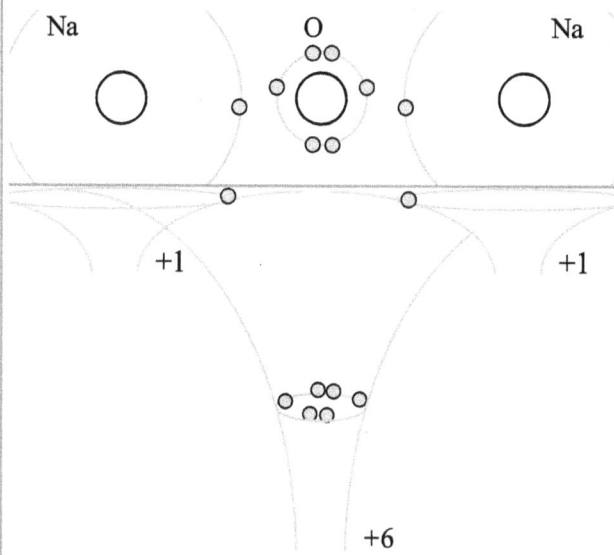

2. A small pile of magnesium powder and sulfur will ignite in brilliant flash.

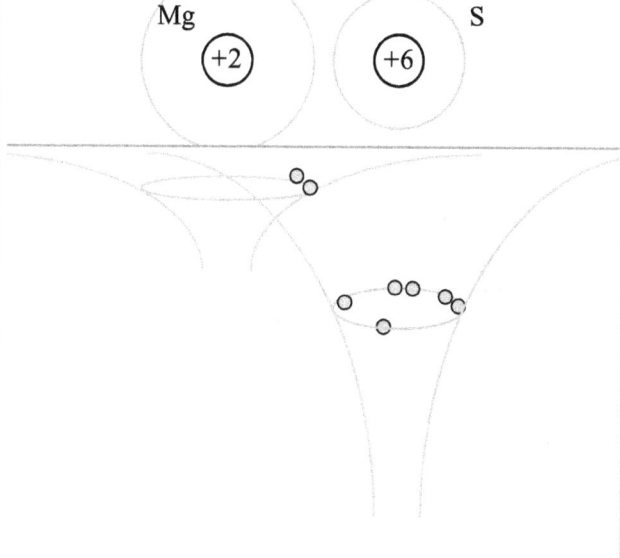

3. Do you think that Mg would release more energy if it burned in sulfur, or in oxygen? Why?

4. Mg reacts vigorously with Br to make MgBr$_2$. You will need to add potential wells for Br.

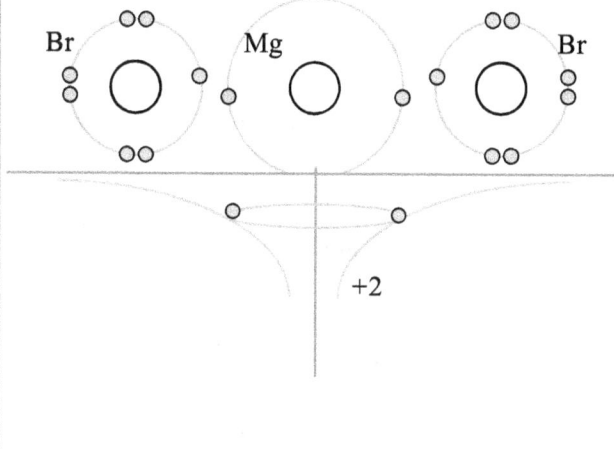

5. Show how electrons move from Na to Cl to make Na$^+$ and Cl$^-$ ions.

Then sketch a few ions in a crystal lattice.

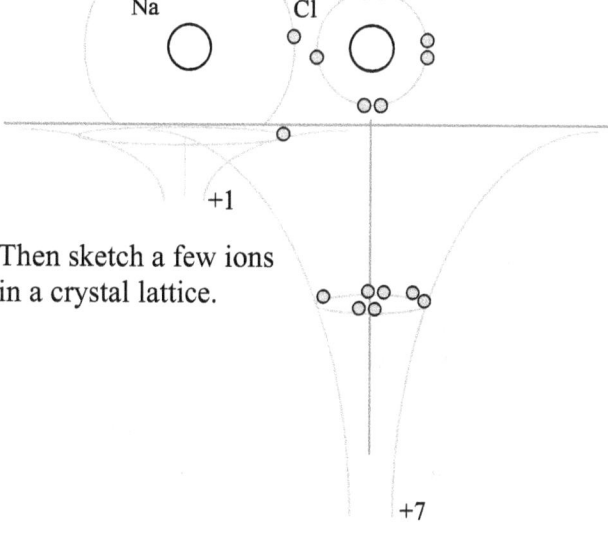

© Ross Lattner Publishing   www.rosslattner.ca

Table Talk
Student Exercises

Electrons and Energy ...

Activity 4.4: The Combustion of Methane

What Are We Thinking About?
- Carbon and hydrogen happen to have their valence electrons at nearly the same potential energy.
- The electrons in methane, CH_4, have potential energies consistent with those of C and H.
- The electrons in oxygen, O_2, have potential energies consistent with those of oxygen.

What's The Question? What happens to the electrons in a compound, such as methane, when the methane is burned in oxygen?

1. Reactants: Methane and Oxygen.

These Ross diagrams show the top view, that is, looking "down the funnel" into the potential energy wells. The electrons of carbon and hydrogen ● are dark grey, and oxygen's ○ are light grey.

2. Products: Carbon Dioxide and Water.

The core - valence - radius diagrams to show that *all* of methane's electrons have moved *closer* to *greater* core charges! Instead of being shared between a +1 and a +4, all electrons are closer to a +6 core charge.

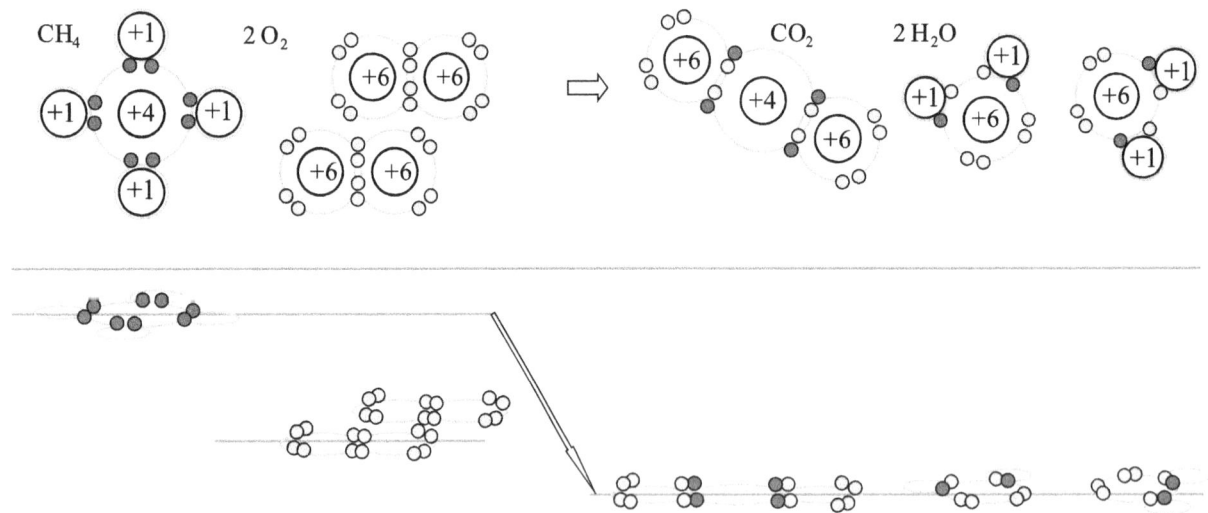

3. CH_4 and O_2 Potential Energy Diagrams

The potential wells have been left out for simplicity. The electrons in the methane molecule ● are shown at a high potential energy level, just below the grey reference line. Those of the oxygen ○ are at a much lower potential energy.

4. CO_2 and H_2O Potential Energy Diagrams

The electrons in carbon dioxide and water are lower in potential energy than they were in either methane or oxygen. Methane's eight electrons have fallen farthest, and account for the energy that heats your homes.

© Ross Lattner Publishing   www.rosslattner.ca

..."Falling" Towards the Core

Name:
Date:

What are we Doing? Acetylene gas, C_2H_2 is also used as a fuel, especially for welding. Each acetylene molecule contains a triple bond, in which the electrons are considerably higher in energy than those in methane. Acetylene is very high on the energy level diagram below. *Why does acetylene produce so much energy as it burns?*

1 Describe the bonding in the Ross diagrams of methane and oxygen	2 Describe how the electrons have changed their arrangements in CO_2 and H_2O.

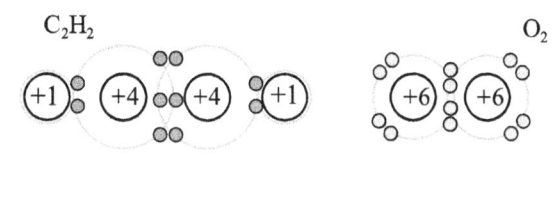

3 Complete the diagram, and describe the electron energy levels in C_2H_2 and O_2	4 Complete the diagram, and describe the change in electron energy level as the products CO_2 and H_2O are formed.

5. Does burning acetylene produce more or less energy than burning methane? Give two different reasons for your answer.

You can say something nice, dear, if you think long enough
How Good is your Table Talk?

Quiz 4: Electrons and Energy

---

1 Draw the valence electrons for sulfur and oxygen at the appropriate energy level.

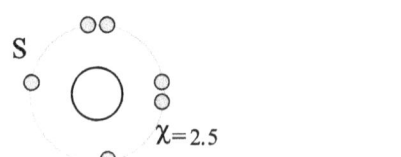

S   χ = 2.5   O   χ = 3.5

+6   +6

Which electrons are lower in potential energy?

Date: _____ / 5

---

2 Hydrogen and helium atoms have similar radii. Draw the valence electrons at the appropriate energy level.

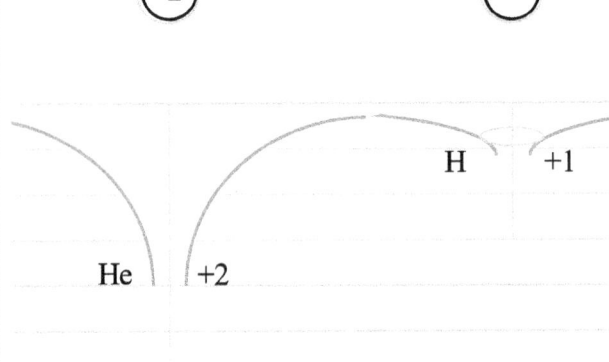

Which electrons are lower in potential energy?

Date: _____ / 5

---

3 Argon and aluminum have the same radius.

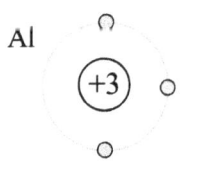 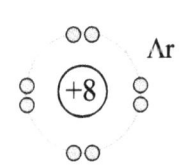

Al   Ar

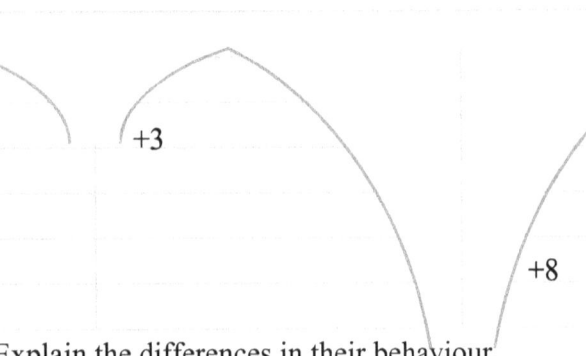

+3   +8

Explain the differences in their behaviour.

Date: _____ / 5

---

4 Complete the core valence radius diagrams for lithium and chlorine.

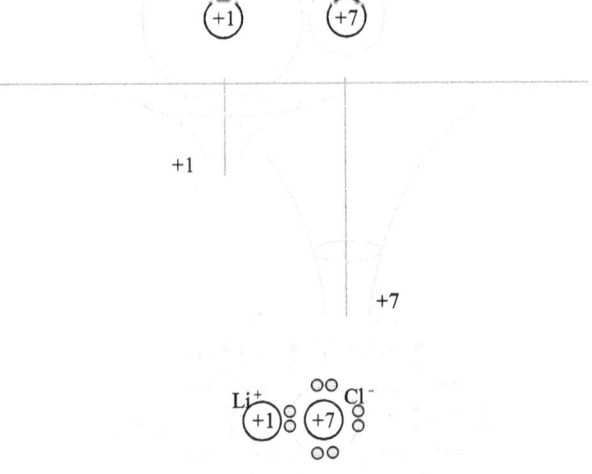

Draw arrows to show electron transfer and energy release with formation of LiCl

Date: _____ / 5

You can say something nice, dear, if you think long enough

How Good is your Table Talk?

Quiz 4: Electrons and Energy   Name:

5   H_2 burns in O_2 with a hot blue flame. Complete Ross and energy level diagrams to show the movement of electrons.

   2 H_2 + O_2 ⟹   2 H_2O

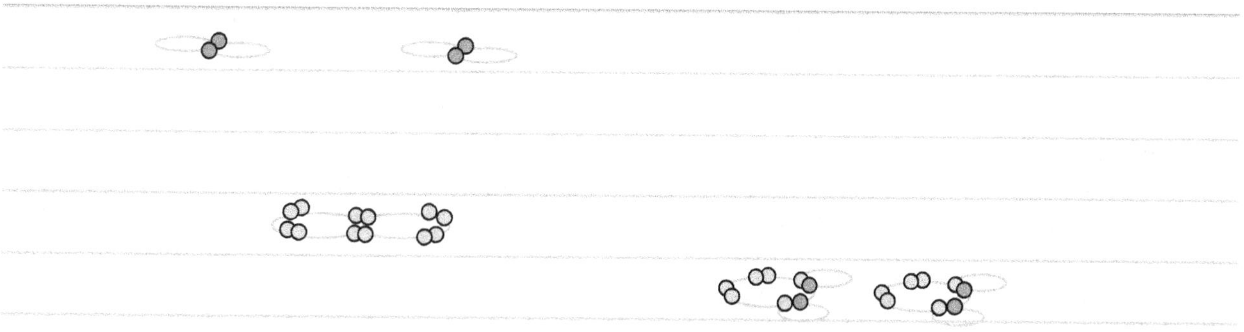

Why does the combustion of hydrogen release so much energy?

Date: / 5

6   Magnesium ribbon will burn in carbon dioxide. In this reaction, the products are magnesium oxide, and a black ribbon of carbon. Write a balanced chemical equation for the reaction:

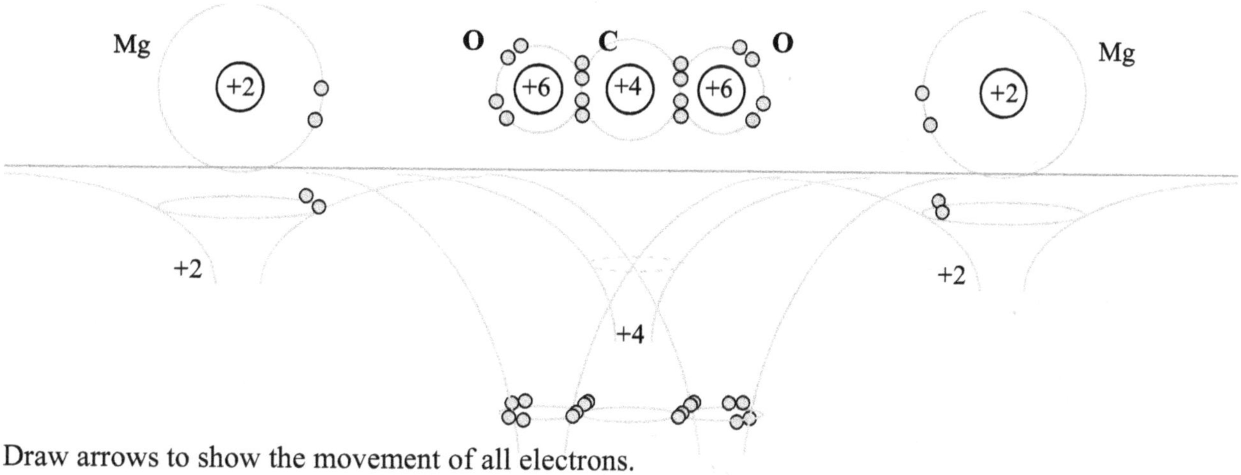

Mg   O   C   O   Mg

Draw arrows to show the movement of all electrons.

Date: / 5

© Ross Lattner Publishing   www.rosslattner.ca

Table Talk
Student Exercises

Polar Bonds ...

Activity 5.1: The Strange Dipolarity of Water

Do You Remember? Valence electrons don't follow smooth circular orbits. Their "path" might be more like a chaotic wandering around the central core charges. The electron's "tracks" are denser in regions where the electron spends more time. The scribbles then represent charge concentration, or a central

	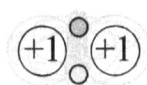	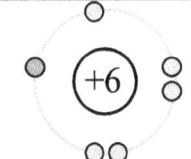	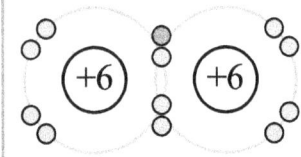
The "path" of an electron, as it swings around hydrogen's +1 core, makes a more or less evenly distributed ball of charge.	In the H$_2$ molecule, the electron spends most of its time midway between the two hydrogen atoms. See the cloud of electron density between the atoms.	What would the "path" of the single electron be around an oxygen atom?	If two oxygen atoms were covalently bonded, where would the electron spend most of its time?

What Are We Thinking About?

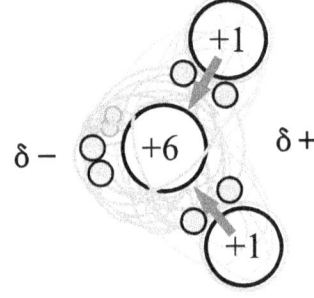

- The four electron pairs around the oxygen atom are distributed in a tetrahedral shape, about 109° apart.
- In the "tug of war" between O and H, oxygen wins, and hydrogen loses.
- The electrons would spend more time close to the +6 core charge of oxygen. The O–H covalent bond must be polar.
- Non-bonding pairs are not involved in a "tug of war" between two atoms. They have no polar character at all.

The H end of the water molecule is more positive. The O end is more negative. The existence of two very polar bonds in such a small molecule makes water a very strong dipole.

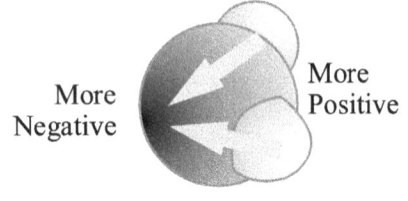

Occasionally, the positive hydrogen atom will come close to one of the non-bonding pairs in another water molecule. The two water molecules can "share" a hydrogen atom, to make a new kind of chemical bond: they "hydrogen bond."

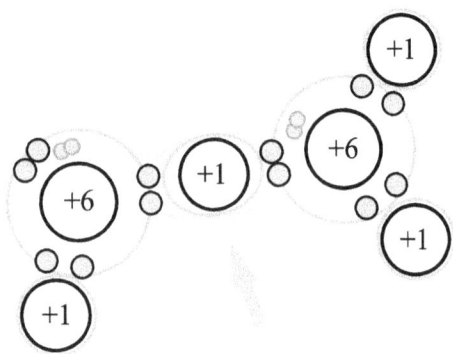

This kind of bond is much weaker than a covalent bond, but is still a very strong force. Hydrogen bonding holds water molecules together in the liquid state, and gives water its very high boiling point.

... and Dipole Molecules

Name:
Date:

What's The Question? Oxygen and hydrogen have very different core charges and atomic radii, making water a highly polar molecule. *How does this affect the behavior of water molecules?*

1. Shown in the diagram are two water molecules. One is a core-valence-radius diagram, the other is a "space-filling" diagram.

   Draw one more molecule of each kind to show how two molecules would attract each other.

   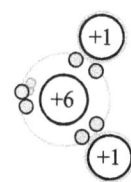
   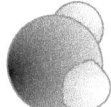

2. A positive potassium ion is attracted to the negative end of one water molecule. Draw four more water molecules to show how they would surround a potassium ion.

   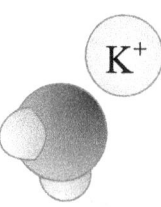

3. A single water molecule is shown with its positive end attracted to a negative chloride ion. Draw five more water molecules to show how they might surround a chloride ion.

   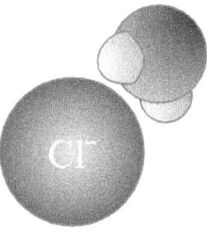

4. Draw 10 more water molecules close together, with the following requirements:
   - 10 instances of dipole-dipole attractions
   - 2 instances of hydrogen bonding.

   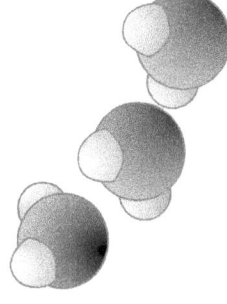

© Ross Lattner Publishing   www.rosslattner.ca

Table Talk
Student Exercises

Polar Bonds ...

Activity 5.2: Alcohols as Dipoles

Do You Remember? Complete the Ross diagrams for H, C and O. Then draw little arrows to indicate which way the electrons will be pulled in each of the covalent bonds in the methanol.

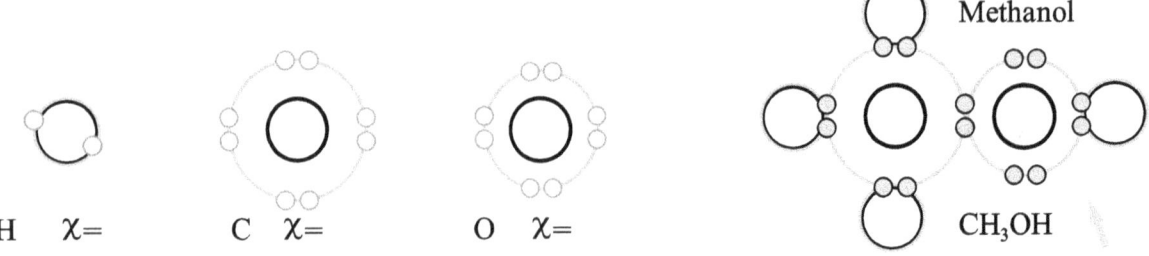

H χ=   C χ=   O χ=

What Are We Thinking About?

- Both carbon and oxygen have four electron pairs around them. Both are tetrahedral in shape. All of the bond angles are about 109 degrees.

- The O–H bond is strongly polar, because the difference in electronegativity is quite large. $\Delta\chi = 1.4$

- The C–O bond is weakly polar. The difference in electronegativity is only $\Delta\chi = 1.0$.

- The C–H bonds are almost non-polar. The difference in electronegativity is very small. $\Delta\chi = 0.4$

Alcohols have both a polar end (the O–H bond) and a non-polar end (the C–H bonds).

They have water-like properties such as high boiling points, soluble in water, and ability to dissolve salts.

They also have oil-like properties, such as solubility in gasoline, and the ability to dissolve oils and waxes.

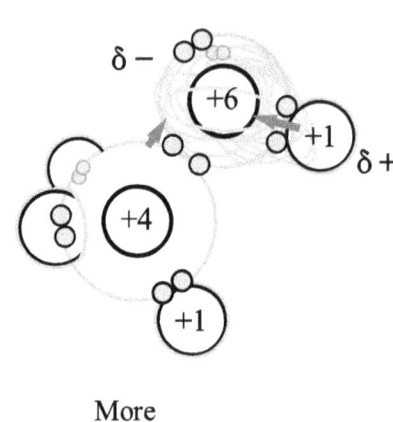

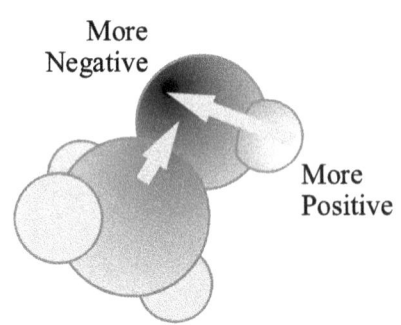

On the next page, you can explore some of the interactions of alcohols with water.

... and Dipole Molecules

Name:
Date:

What's The Question? *How do different alcohols behave in water?*

1. Here are two methanol molecules. One is a Ross diagram, the other is a "space-filling" diagram. Draw one more molecule of each kind. Position them to show the dipole-dipole interactions.

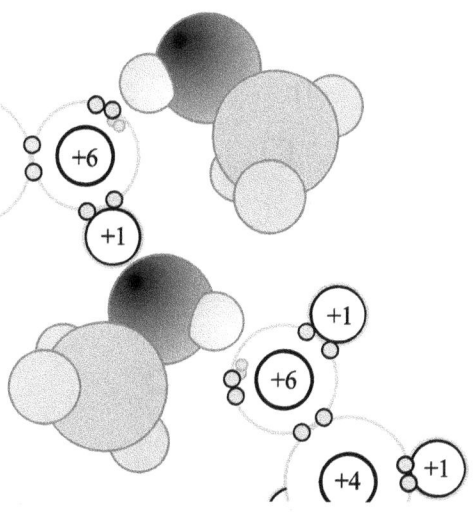

2. Suppose a few drops of methanol were dissolved in a beaker of water. Draw four more water molecules to show how they would interact with the methanol molecule.

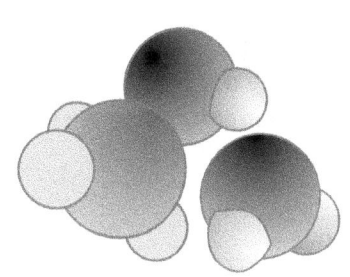

3. Butanol has four carbons. The hydrocarbon end is not polar. Draw two more butanol molecules and describe how they interact with each other.

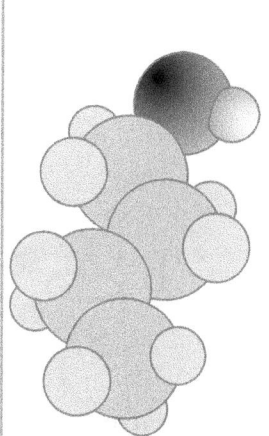

4. Four pentanol molecules are shown. Draw six water molecules to show how they would interact with the alcohol.

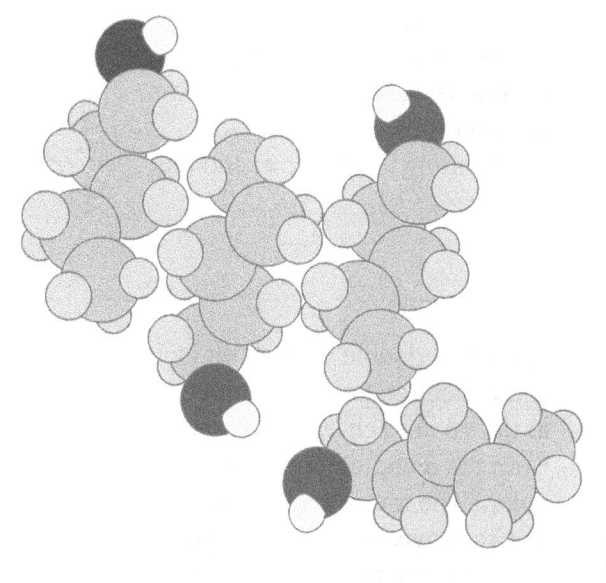

© Ross Lattner Publishing   95   www.rosslattner.ca

Table Talk
Student Exercises

Polar Bonds ...

Activity 5.3: Carbonyl Groups as Dipoles

What Are We Thinking About?
- The *VSEPR* theory is used to explain and predict the geometry of a molecule. Electron pairs around any atom repel each other, and move as far apart as possible around the atom.
- *Orbital overlap* theory is used to explain the characteristics of covalent bonds.
- *Sigma* means *to add*. **S**igma bonds are **S**ingle bonds that *add* two atoms together. Sigma bonds define the geometry of a molecule. They form the **s**igma **s**keleton of the molecule.
- *Pi* bonds are always the second bond. They form above and below the sigma bonds.

- In the water molecule, there are four electron pairs around the oxygen atom. Two are η (non-bonding) pairs. Two are σ (sigma) bonds. The four pairs repel each other into a tetrahedral shape as shown.

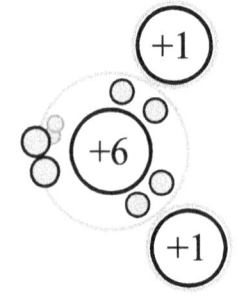 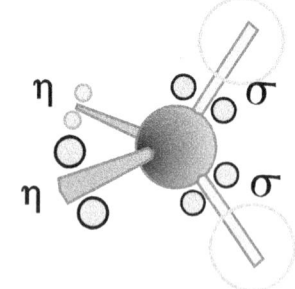

- The oxygen molecule consists of two atoms of oxygen. The first bond between them is a σ bond. The second bond is a π (pi) bond. Every π bond has two clouds, located above and below the plane of the molecule. The two clouds make one π bond.

- Pi bonds arise from overlapping p-type* orbitals. If we represent the bonds as "electron paths," we see clouds of electron density representing the σ, the π, and the η pairs.

One p-type orbital has two halves

Overlapping p-type orbitals make a π bond

- In a C=O double bond, both the σ and π electron pairs are attracted to the +6 core charge of oxygen. Both the σ and the π bonds are polar. The π electrons are more free to move, so a C=O double bond is *more* polar than a C–O single bond.

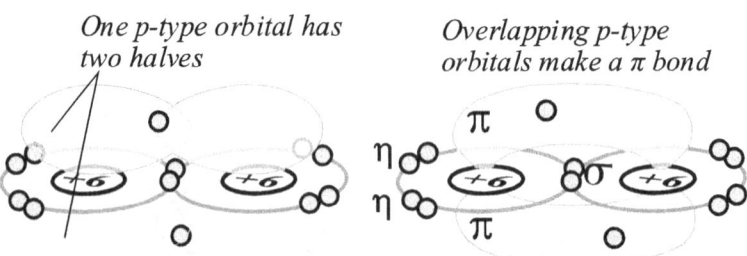

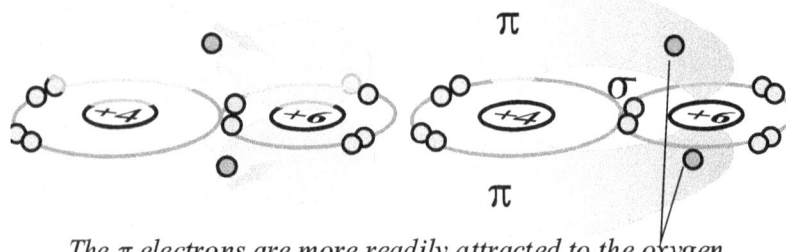

The π electrons are more readily attracted to the oxygen end of the C=O double bond.

* Consult another text for a complete description.

... and Dipole Molecules

Name:
Date:

Focus Question: The C=O group can be found in many organic molecules. It is so frequent, that it is given its own name: the *carbonyl* functional group. *How do the electrons behave in the carbonyl functional groups in organic molecules?*

1. Formaldehyde, H_2CO, has a C=O double bond. Draw **p** orbitals on the C and O atoms, and add two more electrons.

   On the diagram below, trace the "paths" of the moving electrons to indicate electron density clouds.

   Where is the charge density the greatest?

2. Acetone, $CH_3\,CO\,CH_3$ is propane with a carbonyl group on the center carbon atom.

   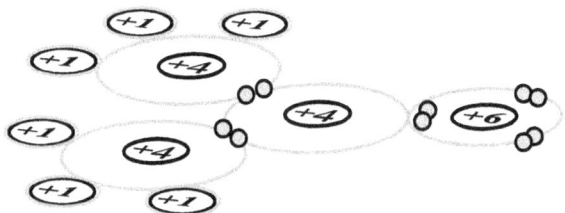

   Complete the diagram by adding the 14 remaining σ and π electrons.

3. You can describe the bonds in acetone as clouds of charge. Draw appropriate "paths" for the electrons to indicate the σ and π regions of electron density. Use different colors to indicate different bonds.

   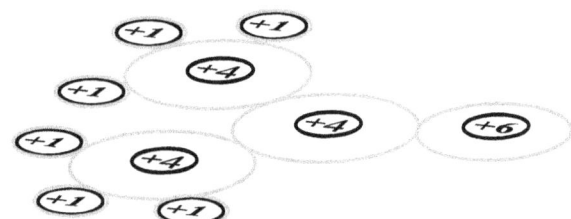

4. All of the σ and η electrons are shown in the ethene molecule, H_2CCH_2 shown below. Draw the p orbitals on the carbon atoms

   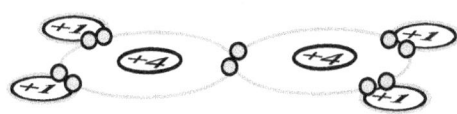

   Now draw the electron clouds

   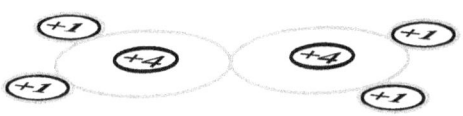

   Is Ethene a dipole? Explain.

You can say something nice, dear, if you think long enough

How Good is your Table Talk?

Quiz 5: Polar Bonds and Dipole Molecules

1. A sodium chloride crystal is dissolving in water. Draw 10 more water molecules. Show how the highly polar water molecules orient themselves around each sodium and chloride ion.

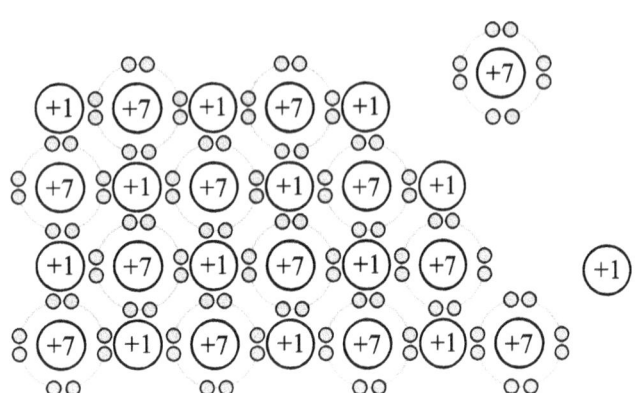

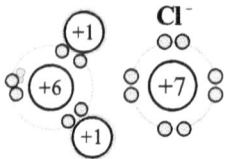

Date: _____ / 5

2. Two glycerine molecules, $CH_2OH-CHOH-CH_2OH$, have dissolved in water. Draw an outline on each glycerine molecule. Draw 10 more water molecules. Orient each water molecule to show dipole-dipole attractions between the water and the glycerine.

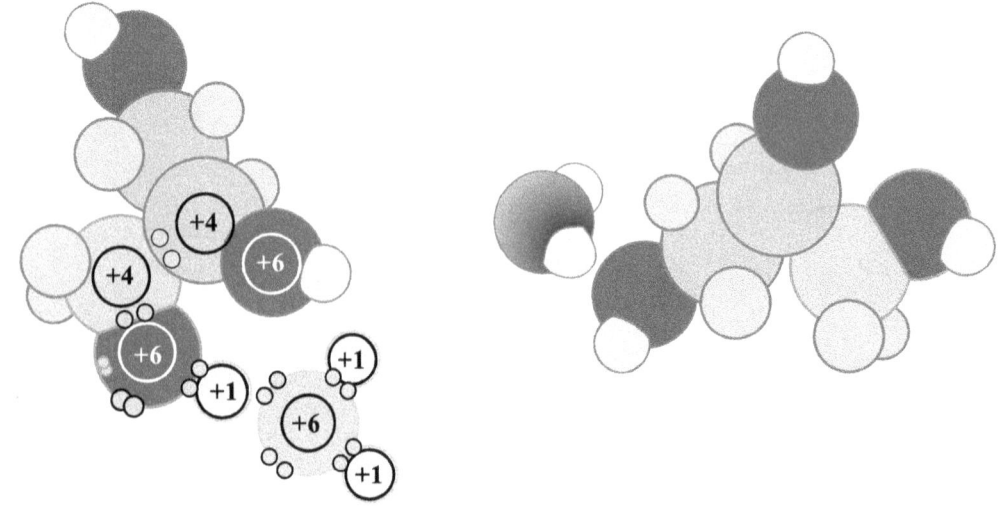

Date: _____ / 5

© Ross Lattner Publishing   98   www.rosslattner.ca

You can say something nice, dear, if you think long enough
How Good is your Table Talk?

Quiz 5: Polar Bonds and Dipole Molecules   Name:

3   Butane is commonly used as a fuel. Butanol is often used in nail polish remover. Label the molecules below. Which one is more soluble in water? Draw 10 water molecules to work out your thoughts, then write a paragraph in the space below.

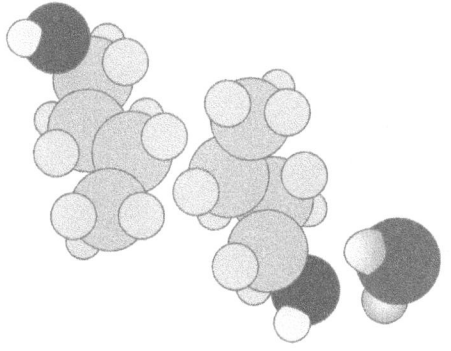
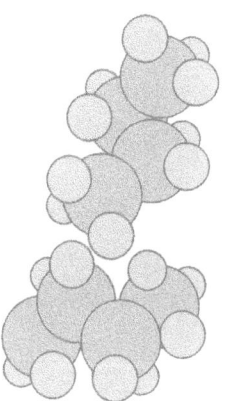

Date: / 5

4   Iodine, I_2, is a dark blue-black crystal. Would a crystal if iodine be soluble in water? Draw as many water molecules and iodine molecules as you need to work out your thoughts. Then answer the question in a paragraph in the space below. (Hint... is water attracted to iodine?)

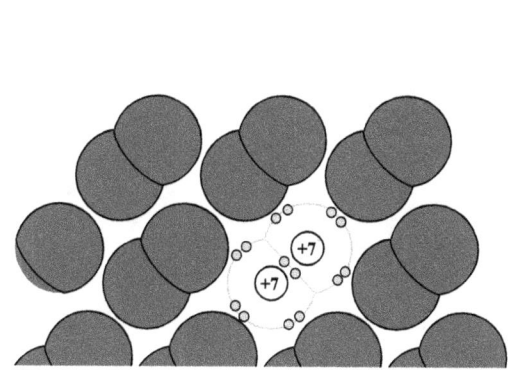
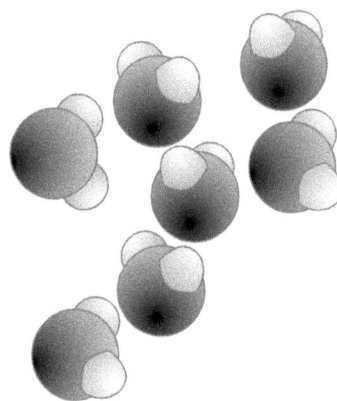

Date: / 5

Quiz 5: Polar Bonds and Dipole Molecules   Name:

5   Butane C_4H_{10}, is commonly used as a fuel. Butanol, C_4H_9OH, is often used in nail polish remover. Both of them can be purchased in the liquid state. Label the molecules below. If you put equal amounts of each liquid on a glass plate, which one would evaporate most quickly? Draw 5 more molecules of each to work out your thoughts.

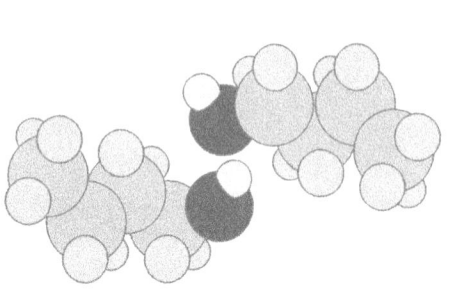
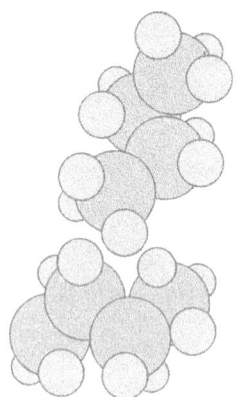

Write a short paragraph to explain your thinking.

Date: / 5

6   Cyclohexane, C_6H_{12}, is a hydrocarbon that used to clean fine machines such as clocks. Draw three more cyclohexane molecules adjacent to these. Indicate any dipole-dipole forces or hydrogen bonds, if they exist.

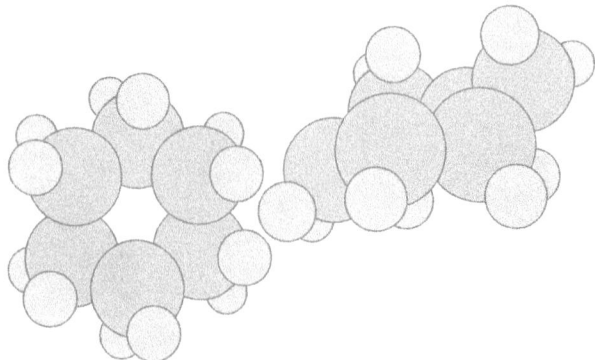

Would cyclohexane require high temperatures to evaporate? Why or why not?

Date: / 5

You can say something nice, dear, if you think long enough

How Good is your Table Talk?

Quiz 5: Polar Bonds and Dipole Molecules   Name:

---

7   Propanone CH_3-CO-CH_3, has a C=O double bond while and 2-propanol, CH_3-CHOH-CH_3, has a C-O single bond. *Does the bonding make a difference in the molecules' dipole character?*

Draw the electrons needed to σ and π bonds. Draw "electron paths" to indicate electron density.

CH_3-CO-CH_3 CH_3-CHOH-CH_3

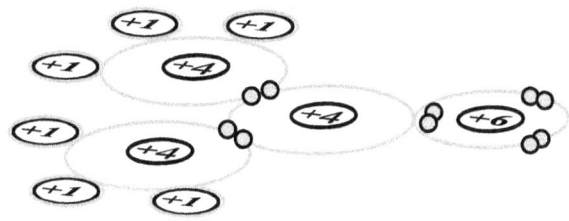   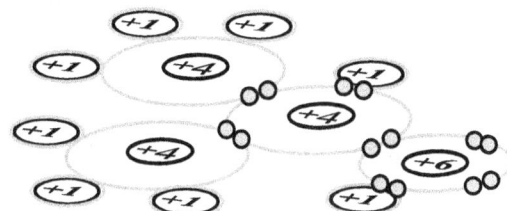

Date: / 5

---

8   Propanone has a boiling point of 56°C. The boiling point of 2-propanol is 82°C. *Why are the boiling points so different?* Draw three more of each molecule to work out your thoughts. Write your answer in a paragraph below the diagrams.

CH_3-CO-CH_3 CH_3-CHOH-CH_3

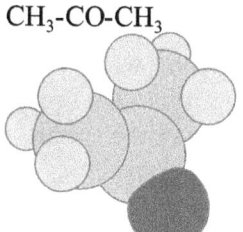   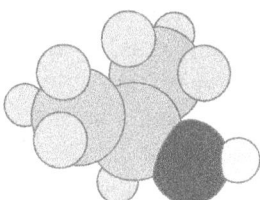

Date: / 5

© Ross Lattner Publishing   101   www.rosslattner.ca

Table Talk
Student Exercises

Who Gets the Electron ...

Lab 6.1: Reactions of Non-metal Oxides and Water

Do You Remember? Complete the Ross diagrams for H, C and O and S. Write the value of the electronegativity of each element.

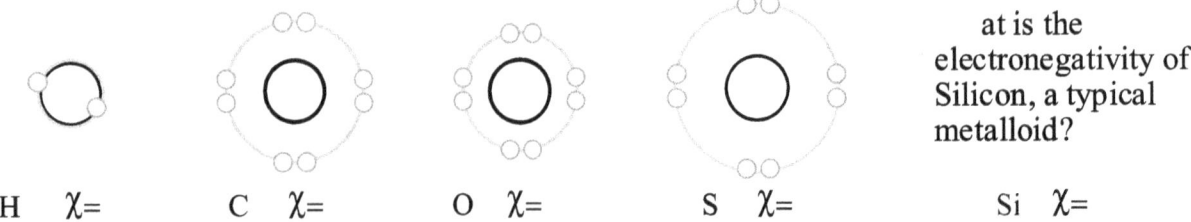

H χ=   C χ=   O χ=   S χ=   Si χ=

What is the electronegativity of Silicon, a typical metalloid?

What's The Question? Carbon, sulfur and oxygen are all non-metals. *Will carbon oxide produce an acid or a base? Will sulfur oxide produce an acid or a base?*

What Are We Doing?
1. **Predict** an answer, and **Explain** your prediction.
    Caution: hot objects and danger of burns.
    Caution: SO_2 is noxious! Use a small quantity of sulfur, the size of a rice grain.

2. Fill two gas bottles with oxygen gas, and cover them with glass plates. Add 1 cm of water, plus 10 drops of bromthymol blue.

3. Place 4 - 6 small lumps of charcoal (carbon) in the deflagrating spoon, and heat it in a Bunsen flame until it is red hot. Gently lower the spoon into the oxygen. Do not touch the water! Raise and lower the spoon slowly to stir up the oxygen.

4. Observe the reaction for 2 min, then withdraw the spoon, close the gas bottle, and gently swirl the bromthymol blue solution.

5. Put a very small (rice-grain size) piece of sulfur in the spoon. Gently warm it in the Bunsen burner flame until it just catches fire. Quickly lower it into the second gas bottle of fresh oxygen. Do not touch the water! Raise and lower the spoon slowly to stir up the oxygen.

6. Observe the reaction for 2 min. Withdraw the spoon, close the gas bottle, and gently swirl the bromthymol blue solution.

Questions For Later...
1. What evidence do you have that an acid or base was produced?

2. Sulfur dioxide is produced in mining, manufacturing, and in the use of sulfur bearing gasoline. What products would be formed if sulfur dioxide was present in rain clouds? Explain.

© Ross Lattner Publishing   www.rosslattner.ca

... Metals, Non-Metals and pH

Name:
Date:

Focus Question: Write the question that you are trying to answer.

1	**Predict:** will carbon dioxide and sulfur dioxide produce acids or bases?	2	**Explain** your thinking.
3	**Observe** the reactions. Were your predictions correct?	4	**Explain**, using any new ideas that you gained from this experiment.

After the experiment...
Complete this diagram to show four different representations of the chemical change you observed.

____ S + ____ O_2 ⇒ ____ SO_2

Sulfur + _____ ⇒ Sulfur Dioxide

____ g + ____ g = ____ g

After the experiment...
Complete this diagram to show four different representations of the chemical change you observed.

____ C + ____ O_2 ⇒ ____ CO_2

Carbon + _____ ⇒ _____

____ g + ____ g = ____ g

In each case, the oxide reacts with water to form an acid.

____ CO_2 + ____ H_2O ⇒ ____ H_2CO_3

____ SO_2 + ____ H_2O ⇒ ____ H_2SO_3

Table Talk
Student Exercises
Who Gets the Electron ...

Activity 6.2: What Makes Non-metal Oxides Acidic?

Do You Remember? Complete the Ross diagrams for H, C, O and S. Write the electronegativity of each element.

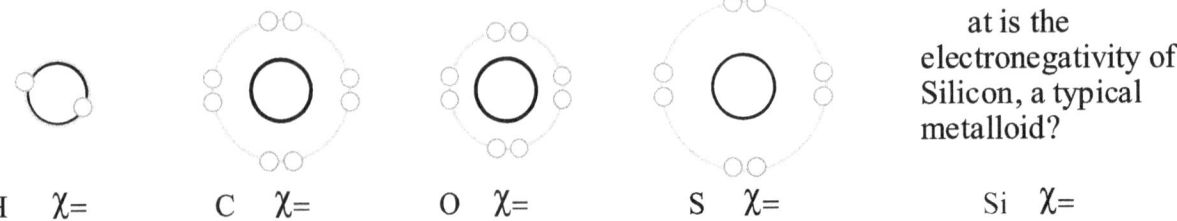

H χ=   C χ=   O χ=   S χ=   Si χ=

at is the electronegativity of Silicon, a typical metalloid?

What Are We Thinking About?
- In a covalent bond between different atoms, the "tug of war" for the electrons is not equal.

- Hydrogen has χ = 2.1. Silicon has χ = 1.8. In other words, hydrogen's χ lies on the dividing line between metals and non-metals.

- An acidic solution contains H⁺ ions. (hydrogen ions).

What Are We Doing? The molecule at right is H_2CO_3, made by dissolving CO_2 in water. Complete the diagram as follows.

1. Write the core charge in the each atom, as shown.

2. Write the electronegativity (χ) near each atom, as shown.

3. Draw clouds of charge density, as shown.

4. Draw arrows to show the movement of electrons in the bonds.

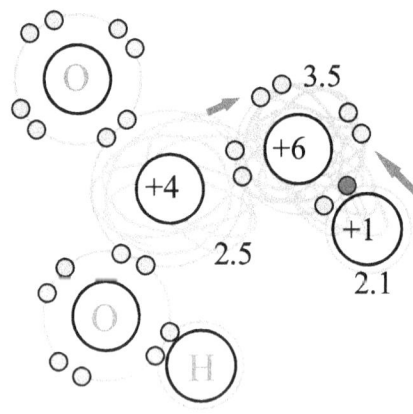

Questions for Later... Answer these questions for each problem, including the example above.

1. Which element has the lowest χ ? That element will "lose" electrons to the others, and will have the lowest charge density around it. What kind of ion will it become?

2. Which element has the greatest χ ? That element will always "win" electrons from the others. It is "the big winner" of electrons, and has the greatest charge density around it..

3. Which element forms a persistent covalent bond with the "big winner?"

... Metals, Non-Metals and pH

Name:
Date:

What are we doing? Complete each diagram as in the example on previous page.
Questions for later... Then answer all three questions for each diagram as on previous page.

1 Nitric acid HNO_3

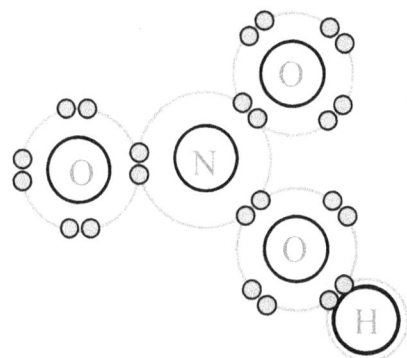

2 Sulfurous acid H_2SO_3

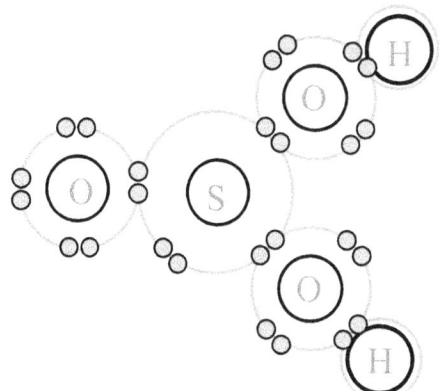

3 Phosphoric acid H_3PO_4

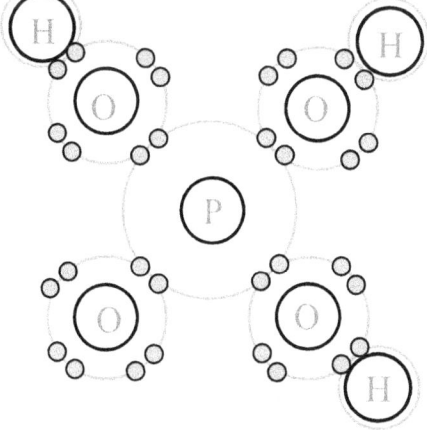

4 Sulfuric acid H_2SO_4

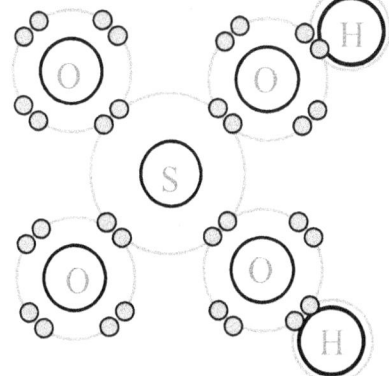

© Ross Lattner Publishing   www.rosslattner.ca

Table Talk
Student Exercises

Who Gets the Electron ...

Lab 6.3: Reactions of Metal Oxides and Water

Do You Remember? Complete the Ross diagrams for H, O, Mg and Ca. Write the value of the electronegativity of each element.

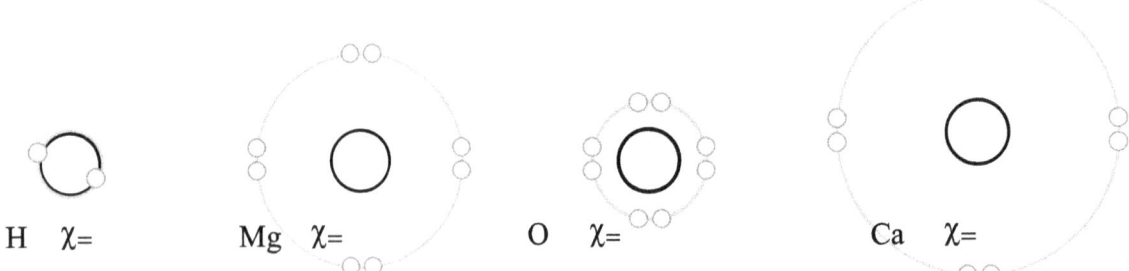

H χ=   Mg χ=   O χ=   Ca χ=

What's The Question? Magnesium and calcium are all metals. *Will magnesium oxide solution be an acid or a base? Will calcium metal produce an acid or a base?*

What Are We Doing?
1. **Predict** an answer, and **Explain** your prediction.

Part A: Your teacher may do this as a demonstration.

2. Fill a gas bottle with oxygen, and cover it with a glass plate. Add 1 cm of water, plus 10 drops of bromthymol blue plus one drop of 0.1 M HCl.

3. Grip a 3 cm piece of magnesium ribbon in with tongs. Ignite the Mg in a Bunsen burner flame. **Caution**: hot objects and danger of burns. Plunge the Mg into the oxygen. **Caution:** very bright light. Do not look directly at the flame. Shield your eyes with a sheet of paper.

4. When the reaction is over, let the ash fall into the water. Withdraw the tongs, close the bottle, and gently swirl the bromthymol blue solution.

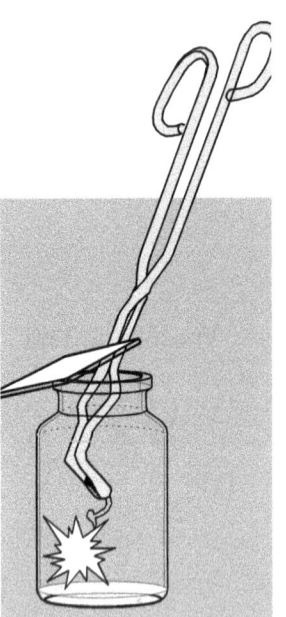

Part B: Your teacher may do this as a demonstration.

5. Add 1 cm of water, 10 drops of bromthymol blue and 1 drop of 0.1 M HCl to a 125 mL Erlenmeyer flask. **Caution:** use a small flask, 125 mL.

6. Add 2 small pieces of Ca to the water. Cover the flask with a wire gauze. It may take a few minutes for the reaction to begin.

7. Test the gas by bringing a burning splint to the mouth of the flask.

Questions For Later...
1. What evidence do you have that an acid or base was produced?

2. Limestone is calcium carbonate. Would limestone soils be acidic or basic? Explain.

... Metals, Non-Metals and pH

Name:
Date:

Focus Question: Write the question that you are trying to answer.	
1 **Predict:**	2 **Explain** your thinking.
3 **Observe** the reactions. Were your predictions correct?	4 **Explain**, using any new ideas that you gained from this experiment.

After the experiment...
Complete this diagram to show four different representations of the chemical change you observed.

____ Mg + ____ O₂ ⇒ ____ MgO

Magnesium + _____ ⇒ Magnesium Oxide

____ g + ____ g = ____ g

Complete this diagram to show four different representations of the chemical change.

____ MgO + ____ H₂O ⇒ ____ Mg(OH)₂

Magnesium Oxide + _____ ⇒ Magnesium Hydroxide

____ g + ____ g = ____ g

Complete this diagram to show four different representations of the chemical change.

____ Ca + ____ H₂O ⇒ ____ H₂ + ____ Ca(OH)

Calcium + _____ ⇒ _____ + Calcium Hydroxide

____ g + ____ g = ____ g + ____ g

© Ross Lattner Publishing   107   www.rosslattner.ca

Table Talk
Student Exercises

Who Gets the Electron ...

Activity 6.4: What Makes Metal Oxides Basic?
Do You Remember? Complete the Ross diagrams for H, O, Mg and Ca. Write the value of the electronegativity of each element.

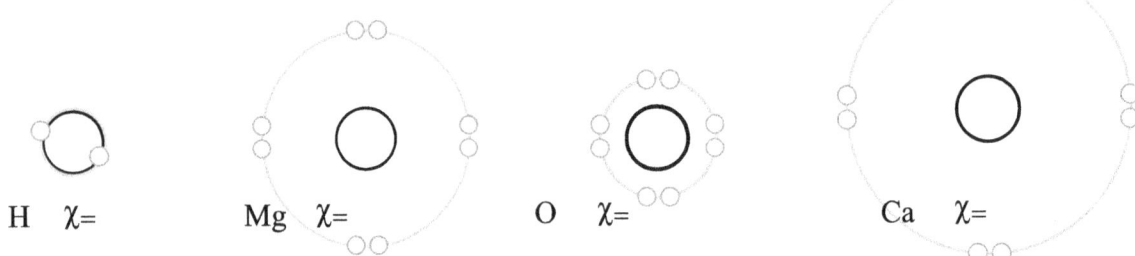

H χ=   Mg χ=   O χ=   Ca χ=

What's The Question? Metal oxides formed basic solutions when they dissolved in water. *Why? What is it about the group 2 metals that makes them become basic?*

What Are We Thinking About?
- In a covalent bond between different atoms, the "tug of war" for the electrons is not equal.

- Hydrogen has χ = 2.1, which is greater than that of the alkali metals. Hydrogen is capable of taking electrons from the metal.

- A basic solution contains OH⁻ ions. (hydroxide ions).

What Are We Doing? MgO and H_2O are shown at right.

1. Write the core charge in the core of each atom

2. Write the electronegativity (χ) near each atom.

3. Draw clouds of charge density, as shown.

4. Draw arrows to show the movement of electrons.

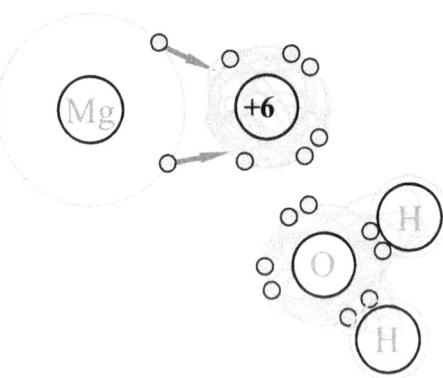

Questions for Later... Answer these questions for each problem, including the example above.

1. *Which element has the lowest χ ?* That element is "the big loser." It will "lose" electrons to the others, and will have the lowest electron density around it.

2. *Which element has the greatest χ?"* This element always "wins" electrons, and has the greatest electron density. It's "the big winner."

3. *Which element is in the middle?* Hydrogen! It will either form a covalent bond with itself H_2, or with oxygen as hydroxide, OH⁻. *Write the names and chemical formulas of all of the products.*

© Ross Lattner Publishing   www.rosslattner.ca

… **Metals, Non-Metals and pH**

Name:
Date:

What are we doing? Complete each diagram as in the example on previous page.
Questions for later... Then answer all three questions for each diagram as on previous page.

1   Sodium oxide and water: $Na_2O + H_2O$

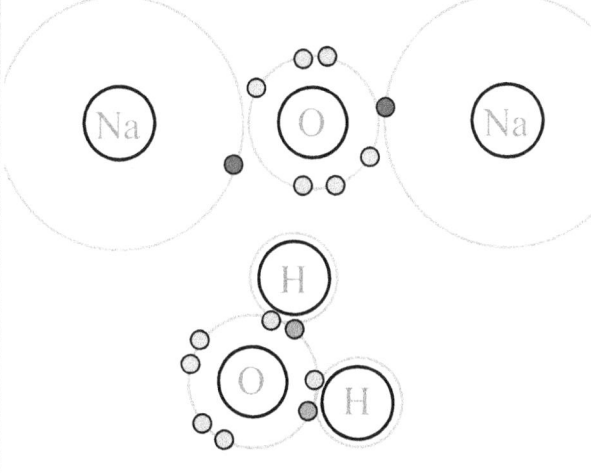

2   Calcium and water: $Ca + H_2O$

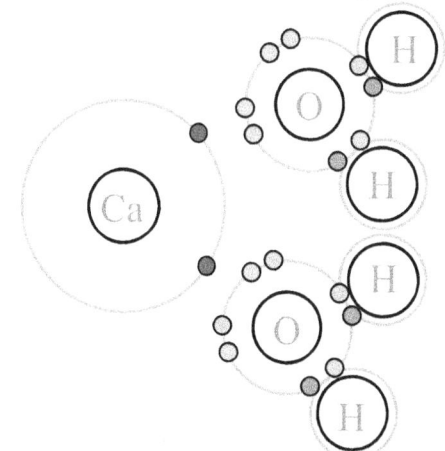

3   Lithium plus water: $Li + H_2O$

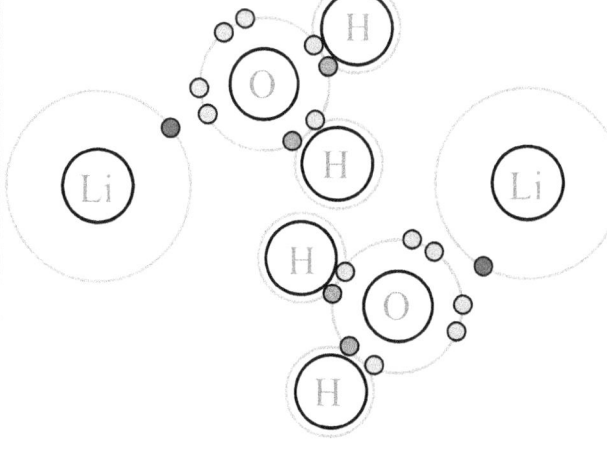

4   Barium Oxide and water: $BaO + H_2O$

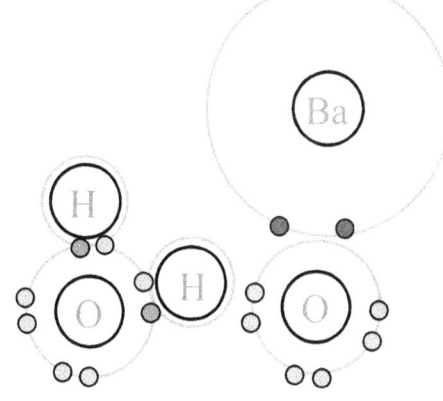

© Ross Lattner Publishing   www.rosslattner.ca

Table Talk
Student Exercises

Who Gets the Electron ...

Activity 6.5: Oxidation and Acid Strength

What's The Question? Acids that are not 100% dissociated are called *weak acids*. These exist in an equilibrium system, in which the acid constant K_a is the equilibrium constant. The greater the K_a, the stronger the acid. *How can we use the Ross model to predict acid strength?*

What Are We Thinking About?
- Oxy acids have the formula H_nXO_m, (**X** is a non-metal atom, and **n** and **m** are integers.)
- The greater **X**'s core charge and the smaller its radius, the stronger the oxy acid. That is equivalent to saying " the greater **X**'s electronegativity, the stronger the oxy acid."
- The greater the oxidation number ⦸ of **X** , the stronger the oxy acid
- Each additional oxygen pulls **X**'s electrons outward and away from the hydrogen. The more polar the O–H bond, the more likely H^+ can break off, and the stronger the acid.

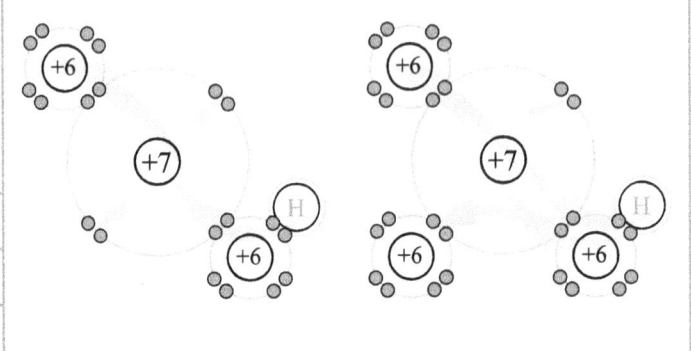

Iodic acid has one more oxygen than iodous acid. As the iodine becomes more highly oxidized, electrons are more strongly pulled away from the hydrogen.

Acid	χ_x	⦸$_x$	K_a
Iodous HIO_2	2.5	+3	3×10^{-5}
Iodic HIO_3	2.5	+5	2×10^{-1}

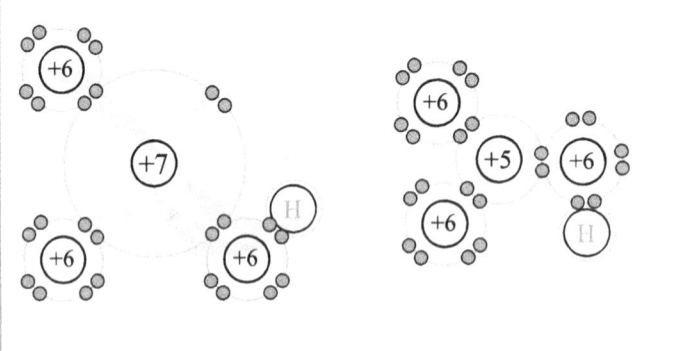

Nitric and iodic acid have similar chemical formulas. Both have ⦸$_x$ = +5. N is much smaller than I, and more electronegative.

Acid	χ_x	⦸$_x$	K_a
Nitric HNO_3	3.0	+5	200
Iodic HIO_3	2.5	+5	2×10^{-1}

What Are We Doing? For the examples above, and the questions on the following page:

1. On each X : O bond, draw an arrow to indicate the movement of X's electrons (see examples).
2. Write the oxidation number ⦸ on the X atom in each case (see examples).
3. Complete the table with information as shown in examples.
4. Explain why one of the acids in each pair is significantly stronger than the other.

... Metals, Non-Metals and pH

Name:
Date:

Acid	χ_x	$\varnothing_x$	K_a
Sulfurous H_2SO_3			2×10^{-2}
Sulfuric H_2SO_4			$2 \times 10^{+6}$

Acid	χ_x	$\varnothing_x$	K_a
Nitric HNO_3			200
Nitrous HNO_2			2×10^{-4}

Acid	χ_x	$\varnothing_x$	K_a
Carbonic H_2CO_3			4×10^{-7}
Sulfurous H_2SO_3			2×10^{-2}

Acid	ϵ_x	$\varnothing_x$	K_a
Nitric HNO_3			200
Chloric $HClO_3$			10

Question for Later... On some of the examples above, the central atom X has one or two non-bonding pairs. Does the presence of a non-bonding pair affect the K_a? Give reasons for your answer.

© Ross Lattner Publishing   www.rosslattner.ca

You can say something nice, dear, if you think long enough

How Good is your Table Talk?

Quiz 6: Acids and Bases

1. In the list below are six oxides. Check off *only those oxides which will form acids*. Explain your choice.

	MgO	Magnesium Oxide
	SiO$_2$	Silicon Oxide
	SeO$_2$	Selenium Oxide
	P$_2$O$_5$	Phosphorus Oxide
	Li$_2$O	Lithium Oxide
	BeO	Beryllium Oxide

   Date: _____ / 5

2. Silicon oxide is the main ingredient in glass. Your drinking glasses at home are made of SiO$_2$. Would silicon dioxide form an acid or base solution in water? Explain.

   Date: _____ / 5

3. Write the symbol and χ for carbon, oxygen and hydrogen on the appropriate atom.

   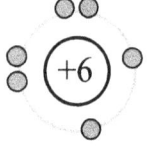 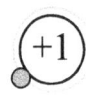

   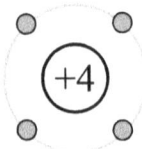

   In the competition for electrons, which element will be the "big winner," the "big loser," and the "covalent middle?" Explain.

   Date: _____ / 5

4. Decide whether water, H$_2$O, is pure covalent, polar covalent, or ionic, and draw the bonding using Ross diagrams.

   Date: _____ / 5

© Ross Lattner Publishing   112   www.rosslattner.ca

You can say something nice, dear, if you think long enough
How Good is your Table Talk?

Quiz 6: Acids and Bases Name:

---

5 Write the symbol for and χ lithium, oxygen and hydrogen on the appropriate atom.

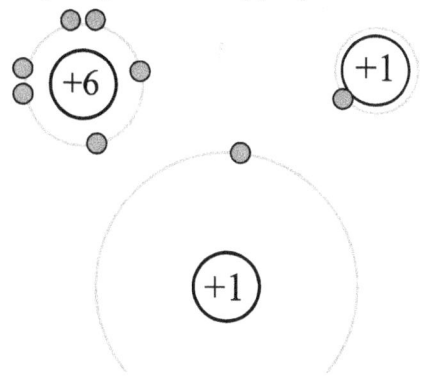

In the competition for electrons, which element will be the "big winner," the "big loser," and the "covalent middle?" Explain.

Date: _____ / 5

---

6 In the list below are six oxides. Check off *only those oxides which will form bases*. Explain your choice.

CaO	Calcium Oxide
CO_2	Carbon Oxide
SO_2	Sulfur Oxide
P_2O_5	Phosphorus Oxide
Na_2O	Sodium Oxide
K_2O	Potassium Oxide

Date: _____ / 5

---

7 Ordinary household bleach is probably one of the strongest acids in your home.

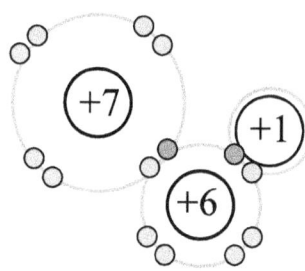

Draw "electron paths" of the two darker electrons to indicate regions of high and low electron density. Then explain why is HOCl an acid.

Date: _____ / 5

---

8 If an element has a small radius, is it *more* likely or *less* likely to behave as an acid? Explain.

Date: _____ / 5

You can say something nice, dear, if you think long enough

How Good is your Table Talk?

Quiz 6: Acids and Bases Name:

9   Selenium is used in dandruff shampoos. Would selenium (IV) oxide form an acid or a base with water?

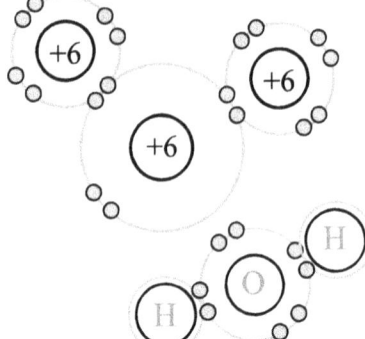

Use the diagram and a paragraph to explain.

Date: _____ / 5

10 Li_2O is mixed with water. Draw arrows to show the movement of electrons in this system. Is it acid or base? Explain.

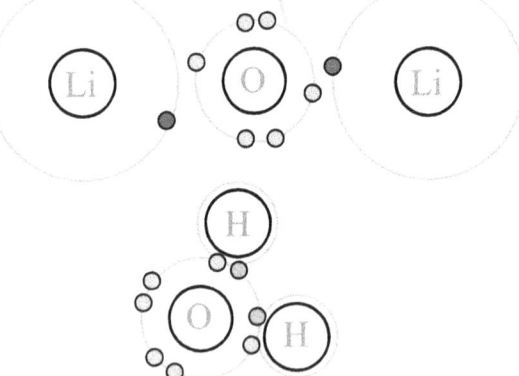

Date: _____ / 5

11 Consider the elements in the non-shaded cells of the table below. Would each element, if shaken with water and oxygen, make an acid, base or neutral mixture? Mark each box **A**cid, **B**ase or **N**eutral.

Explain your choices briefly.

Date: _____ / 5

12 If an element has a large core charge (e.g. +5 or greater), is it more likely to behave as an *acid* or as a *base*? Explain.

Date: _____ / 5

© Ross Lattner Publishing   114   www.rosslattner.ca

You can say something nice, dear, if you think long enough
How Good is your Table Talk?

Quiz 6: Acids and Bases   Name:

13   Nitrous acid and chlorous acid share some features. What acid would have the greatest acid strength, that is, the greatest K_a? Add χ_x and $\varnothing_x$, arrows and any other information you need to work out your thoughts.

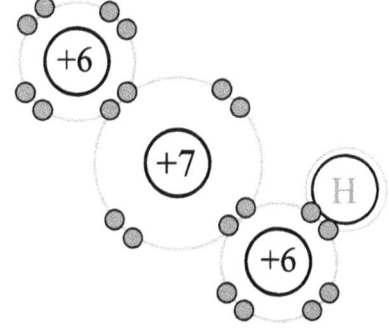 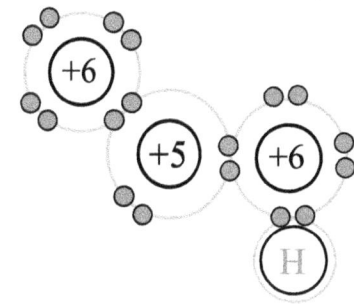

Write a short paragraph to explain your thinking.

Date: / 5

14   Carbonic acid, H_2CO_3, has acid constant $K_a = 4 \times 10^{-7}$. Acetic acid, CH_3COOH, is a much stronger acid with $K_a = 2 \times 10^{-5}$. Why is acetic acid so much more acidic than carbonic acid? Add χ_x and $\varnothing_x$, arrows and any other information you need to work out your thoughts.

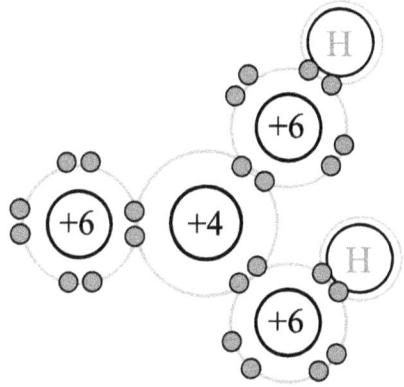 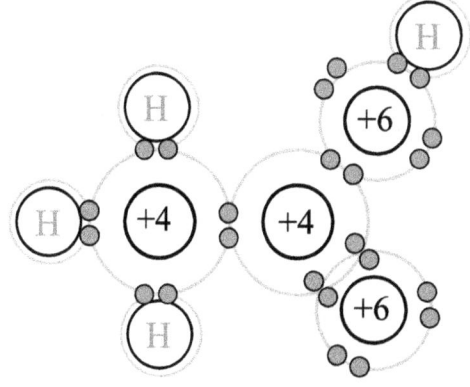

Write a short paragraph to explain your thinking.

Date: / 5

© Ross Lattner Publishing   115   www.rosslattner.ca

www.ingramcontent.com/pod-product-compliance
Lightning Source LLC
Chambersburg PA
CBHW080405170426
43193CB00016B/2819